CUBA
Talking about revolution

CUBA
Talking about revolution

Conversations with
Juan Antonio Blanco
by Medea Benjamin

OCEAN

A project of Global Exchange

Cover design by David Spratt
Cover screenprint by Raúl Martínez (courtesy of Editorial José Martí)

ISBN 1-875284-97-4

First edition 1994
Second edition 1997

Printed in Australia

Published by Ocean Press
Australia: GPO Box 3279, Melbourne, Victoria 3001, Australia
• Fax: (61-3) 9329 5040 • E-mail: edit@oceanpress.com.au
USA: PO Box 834, Hoboken, NJ 07030

in association with Global Exchange
2017 Mission Street, #303, San Francisco, CA 94110, USA

OCEAN PRESS DISTRIBUTORS
United States & Canada: LPC/InBook,
    1436 West Randolph St, Chicago, IL 60607, USA
Britain and Europe: Global Book Marketing,
    38 King Street, London, WC2E 8JT, UK
Australia and New Zealand: Astam Books,
    57-61 John Street, Leichhardt, NSW 2040, Australia
Cuba and Latin America: Ocean Press,
    Calle 21 #406, Vedado, Havana, Cuba
Southern Africa: Phambili Agencies,
    PO Box 28680, Kensington 2101, Johannesburg, South Africa

www.oceanbooks.com.au

Introduction
by Medea Benjamin

Looking at U.S. policy toward Cuba, you would think the Cold War was still raging. The United States not only continues its three-decade-old policy of embargoing and isolating Cuba, but has even tightened the restrictions on trade with Cuba.

Global Exchange, one of the U.S. organizations trying to end the Cold War against Cuba, has been organizing monthly study seminars to Cuba and bringing Cubans on speaking tours to the United States to help bridge the gap between the two nations. We are constantly looking for Cubans who have the delicate skills it takes to speak to foreign visitors in terms they can understand, given that they come from such different worlds and operate under such different mindsets. Juan Antonio Blanco, whose voice you will hear in this book, is one of the Cubans most able to bridge this gap.

A look at his background explains why. To start with, Juan Antonio studied at an American school in Havana before the revolution, where he not only learned to speak terrific English, but also learned how to relate to people of different cultures and classes. He later studied history and got a doctorate in philosophy, so he can draw on his rigorous academic background to put issues into a larger historical and philosophical context. His years of working as a diplomat at the United Nations, where he represented Cuba in the Nonaligned Movement, honed his ability to deal with people of radically different political persuasions without losing his cool.

Finally, Juan Antonio is an ardent supporter of the Cuban revolution and is a member of Cuba's Communist Party, but he speaks with an independent voice. After years of working as an analyst with the Central Committee of the Communist Party, Juan

Antonio asked to leave and form his own non-governmental organization to study ethics and politics. At that time, in 1992, this was something virtually unheard of. The only non-governmental organizations in Cuba (meaning organizations that get no financial support from the government) were churches and dissident groups. But Juan Antonio was determined to have an independent voice, and after jumping through numerous bureaucratic hoops, he was able to start his own "think tank" to study politics and ethics.

Named the Félix Varela Center after a 19th century Catholic priest whose teachings set the intellectual underpinning of Cuba's independence struggles, the Center operates out of Juan Antonio's home on a shoestring budget of donations from foreign friends. While most Cubans are caught up in dealing with the day-to-day emergencies of Cuba's present economic crisis, Juan Antonio and his collaborators are focusing on the long-term issues of what socialism and revolution mean in the "new world order."

Given Juan Antonio's great analytical and communication skills, we at Global Exchange invited him to come to the United States on a 14-city speaking tour in April 1993. The problem with such invitations is that the U.S. State Department, as part of its policy of isolating Cuba, often denies visas to visiting Cubans. We solicited the visa for Juan Antonio months in advance, called the State Department endless times, and received letters of support from top universities all over the country. As the tour date approached and we still had no visa, we started to panic. The State Department kept us in suspense literally until the day before his departure date — a technique obviously designed to discourage people from inviting Cubans. But the visa was finally granted and the tour was on.

Juan Antonio spent the next month crisscrossing the country giving lectures, meeting with U.S. government officials, being interviewed by journalists and visiting with non-governmental organizations. I accompanied him for most of this exhausting journey, and at the end of the month we figured out that he had given a total of 90 presentations!

This book evolved from those talks, as well as from late night conversations we had about Cuba's future. During these discussions, I tried to press Juan Antonio on some of his ideas that I found difficult to grasp. My own background with Cuba is that I lived there in the late 1970s and early 1980s, and while I gained a tremendous appreciation for the gains of the revolution in terms of health, education, racial harmony, and egalitarian spirit, I was at the same time worried about the quashing of individual initiative in the economic sphere and the narrowness of political debate. So Juan Antonio and I had some heated discussions over such critical issues as whether or not a one-party state can really accommodate a healthy variety of viewpoints, or why Fidel Castro — if he is indeed so popular — just doesn't call a presidential election. And while Juan Antonio and I often disagreed, the dialogue was always one of respect and camaraderie.

One thing I have learned about Juan Antonio is that he is impossible to label. When he was introduced as a reformist at one of his talks, he immediately corrected his host. "I am not a reformist," he insisted, "I am a radical." Some of his ideas might be considered reformist — he believes Cuba needs more private enterprise, he advocates a more open press. In other areas he sounds like a hardline "conservative". He defends a one-party system and the government's treatment of dissidents, and does not want to see the free market as the motor force of the economy. But he is also an idealist. His hero is Che Guevara, and he continues to believe in the possibility of creating Che's vision of "el hombre nuevo," a person driven by moral convictions and a thirst for social justice rather than by greed and selfishness. Finally, Juan Antonio often comes across as an open-minded "liberal", someone strongly committed to cultural diversity and individual freedoms, including gay rights. He waxes nostalgic about the 1960s and his days as a rock singer, and takes pride in the fact that his teenage son is a rock singer today. (The best time we spent during the speaking tour were the long drives, belting out old Beatles and Elvis Presley songs. Juan Antonio knew all the words, had a beautiful voice, and never missed a beat.)

In sum, Juan Antonio is no stereotypical middle-aged communist. In that sense, he is indeed a "typical" Cuban, for Cuban revolutionaries tend to be much more complex and sophisticated than the Western press makes them out to be. A reformist, a hard-liner, a radical, an idealist, a pragmatist, a futuristic historian, Juan Antonio is a fascinating product of a fascinating nation. This book presents an all-too-rare opportunity to hear the voice of one of Cuba's leading intellectuals. I hope you enjoy our conversations as much as I have enjoyed putting them together.

Remembering the past

Before we begin discussing the Cuban revolution itself, why don't you give us a bit of your own background. I know that you were only about 11 years old when the revolution triumphed in 1959. When did you first grasp what the revolution was all about and when did you make a conscious decision to support the process?

In the years right before the revolution, I was going to a bilingual American school in Cuba, which is where I learned English. My parents sent me to this school because it gave students a good education at a relatively low price, and at that time the Cuban public school system was a total wreck.

The school was run by Americans who were white, southern, religious and very racist. Many of my classmates were sons and daughters of American officials in Cuba. Some of their parents worked for the American Embassy, others for the CIA or as advisers to the Cuban army. The other Cubans studying there were basically middle class.

What about your parents? What were their political views?

I was living between two worlds. In school I was exposed to an upper and middle-class environment and very conservative attitudes. At home I learned exactly the opposite of everything I was hearing in school, because my parents were communists.

How did your parents become communists?

My mother was a self-made woman who started working at age 13. She became politicized while working for the Cuban phone company in the 1930s. There was a big strike and my mother was on a committee to help the striking workers when they were in difficult financial straits. One day a family called her and said they needed some money from the union because they were going hungry. When my mother got to their house, she found that their baby was totally malnourished. She picked up the baby in her arms, and the child died. This experience marked my mother for life and made her swear that she would fight forever against the inequities in Cuban society. She later joined the Communist Party as a way to do that.

In my father's case, he was a poor immigrant from Spain. He was too poor to study, so he became a worker in an American tobacco company. In Cuba, the cigarmakers have traditionally been among the most politicized workers. They were the ones, for example, who supported Martí during the independence struggle. So my father became politicized, too, and like my mother, he joined the Communist Party as a way to change the corrupt and unjust system we had at that time.

So how did you reconcile your parents views with the views you were taught in school?

It was very difficult. Not only were my parents communists, but they were also atheists. When the religious class in school would start, the teacher would say, "Communists, atheists, and Jews go outside to the playground." And let me tell you, that made for a very interesting crowd out in the playground.

During those years, my life at home was very difficult. My parents were very active in the struggle against the Batista dictatorship and our home was raided 11 times by the police. My parents often appeared on police hit lists and had to hide every time we heard a raid was coming. I have memories of the police barging into our house, like in Nazi Germany, and I always had nightmares that my parents would be killed and I would become an orphan.

Did you ever resent your parents involvement? You know how common it is for the children of communists to become conservatives and vice versa.

In some ways I did. I remember one time telling my mother and father that I was not going to be a communist, because I was a rebellious kid and I didn't want to follow in my parent's footsteps. And my mother very wisely said to me, "Well, you're going to have a hard time. Because we're going to teach you to be a decent person and if you are going to be a decent person, you're going to end up being a communist in one way or another." And I guess that she was right. If you were a decent person living in prerevolutionary Cuba, you had to end up embracing some sort of radical position against such an unfair state of affairs.

I remember very clearly the day I became a revolutionary. I was 10 years old, and it was my best Christmas ever because my parents gave me a puppy. I had been asking for a dog for years, but my father was against it because we lived in an apartment. He finally gave in and I was delighted. So I was playing with my new dog, happy as could be, when a little girl about my age, dressed in rags, came to our door begging for money to buy some food.

I had seen lots of beggars in Havana — that was a common sight in Cuba before the revolution. But it was particularly sad for me to realize that on Christmas night, while I was so well fed and happy, there were other children without food and without a roof over their heads. I realized that one of the happiest nights of my life was also one of the saddest for that girl who had nothing.

That was when I started to put all the pieces of the puzzle together. I started to understand why my parents were political activists, why my house would get raided. And that's when, as a young kid, I realized that like my parents, I, too, was a communist and a revolutionary.

But as a child, you couldn't possibly understand the ideology behind socialism or communism. Did you just see the revolution as an alternative to the corrupt regime of Batista?

Like many other Cubans, I didn't join the revolution because of any political doctrine. I had not read the *Communist Manifesto*; I had not read Karl Marx. But I embraced the revolution because I embraced, as a child, this quest for social justice. We made a revolution because we felt that it was only fair to fight for those who didn't have shelter and those who didn't have anything to eat. We felt it was only fair for everyone to have access to health care and a decent education. So it is this vision that brought me into this revolutionary process and it has sustained me throughout these years more than any of the political doctrines I later studied.

When Americans think of the Cuban revolutionary process, they think of 1959 and the triumph of Fidel Castro's ragtag army against Batista. But Cuban revolutionaries often emphasize that the revolution does not date back to 1959, but to Cuba's movement for independence from Spain in the last century. They cite José Martí, Cuba's founding father, as laying the foundation of today's revolution. In fact, as socialism in most of the world has collapsed and the ideological underpinnings of socialism is on such shaky ground, Cubans seem to be reverting more and more to the nationalist roots of their struggle. As an historian and a philosopher, how do you see the relationship between the independence movement of the 1800s and the more recent revolutionary process?

It is impossible to understand the 1959 revolution without understanding the history of Cuba's struggle for independence and self-identity. More than that, it is impossible to understand the apparent stubbornness of the Cuban revolution in trying to stay its course while surrounded on all sides by capitalist countries if you don't understand our history.

This struggle for independence and self-identity began early in the last century, even before José Martí or Antonio Maceo, our founding fathers, were born. In the first half of the last century there was a Catholic priest named Félix Varela, who was probably the first Cuban promoter of liberation theology. Varela marked Cuban history in a very unique way. If you ask Cubans about Félix Varela, they will say, "He was the one who taught us how to think." More importantly, he taught us how to think as Cubans.

Félix Varela started an intellectual revolution that gave birth to a new generation of Cubans who, for the first time, felt and thought as Cubans. He was the man who taught the teachers of José Martí and the others a new way of thinking about Cuban society from a nationalist perspective. One of the major debates of the last century was whether or not Cuba should become another state of the Union, and Varela was very strongly against annexation by the United States.

After this first intellectual revolution came the political revolution and armed struggle. This first stage of independence — the 10-year war from 1868-1878 — was essentially frustrated and ended up with a peace accord signed with the Spanish government, because it was impossible to continue the war under the conditions which prevailed at that time. More than anything else, the war effort was hurt by the divisions and conflicts among revolutionaries themselves. Since that war, those in favor of independence and social change in the island learned to appreciate the need for unity of the revolutionary forces. The very idea of José Martí of creating one revolutionary party that would merge all the splintered groups came from the sad experience of that 10-year war.

Also, the population and the rebel army were exhausted and had virtually no supplies to keep on fighting. The idea of a peace treaty (called The Pact of Zanjon) started to become attractive to many of the rebels. When the pact was signed, only the rebel leader Antonio Maceo protested the treaty at a place called "Mangos de Baraguá". The Baraguá Protest, as it came to be known, is an example of the undefeated Cuban dignity in a moment of military defeat.

The second war against Spain, which was started by José Martí in 1895, was derailed with the American participation in that war and ended with a U.S. military takeover of the island. So neither of these stages of our struggle succeeded in establishing a truly independent, sovereign nation.

Why did these struggles fail?

You must bear in mind that by the time Cuba began its armed struggle in 1868, virtually all the rest of Latin America was freed from Spain. This meant that all the Spanish armies that had been defeated throughout Latin America began to regroup in Cuba. The Spanish had a huge army in Cuba of about 300,000, while the population of Cuba at that time was only about two million!

The Spanish were seasoned fighters who had learned much from their encounters with San Martín, Sucre, and Bolivar. And they also brought to the island the latest in war technology — rifles, cannon and the rest.

Because Cuba was an island, it was unable to receive the kind of assistance other Latin American independence movements received from Bolivar or Sucre or San Martín. The Cuban independence fighters were alone, fighting against a formidable enemy with a far superior military force.

That is why Cuba has been described as the Vietnam of the last century. And that is why resistance against a major power, under conditions of isolation from the rest of the world, is part of our tradition.

You have been reviewing Cuba's history as a way to understand the revolution of 1959. But there were many Third World countries that fought nationalist wars of independence, with varying degrees of success, without later having socialist revolutions.

Yes, but in the case of Cuba, it was more than a struggle for nationhood. There is a peculiarity in the ideology of our independence struggle as given to us both by Félix Varela, the priest, and José Martí, the major intellectual and protagonist of this struggle. And this peculiarity is that Cuba's struggle for independence not only had a political goal of gaining sovereignty, but also an ethical goal of building a new kind of republic.

By the time Martí started the second war of independence in 1895, he had already lived in the United States for a while. He made many keen observations about the United States, and he felt that democratic institutions were being corroded by the egotism and selfishness building up within U.S. society.

Martí was also unhappy with the road taken by the different *caudillos* and Latin American political leaders at that time. Martí saw that the newly independent republics were copying institutions either from Europe or the United States, rather than building institutions based on the traditions of Latin America. In addition, those republics were not working to build equality or social justice. Instead, they were building new forms of dictatorship and exploitation. New classes were emerging but they were new classes whose principal function was to exploit the masses of those countries.

So in the case of Cuba, the independence movement was not only a political struggle to achieve national sovereignty, but it was also very strongly based on an ethical ideal of social justice. To use José Martí's words, the goal of the revolution was to build a republic with all and for the good of all — "con todos y para el bien de todos".

But the independence war achieved neither independence nor social justice.

Precisely. The United States frustrated our attempt to have a sovereign nation. When Cuba was almost at the point of achieving independence from Spain, the United States intervened. In the changing geopolitical world of that time, Spain was a declining power and the United States was ascending, especially in this hemisphere. The United States was determined to impede real Cuban independence.

The U.S. Marines occupied Cuba until 1902, when we were granted formal independence. In order for the United States to grant us our independence, we had to add a special amendment to our constitution. This amendment was not even written in the congress of Cuba, but by a U.S. senator whose name was Platt. The Platt amendment said that the United States had the right to intervene in Cuba whenever the United States perceived that its interests were in jeopardy. To guarantee that the United States would have the ability to intervene, it established a naval station, the Guantánamo Base, that still exists today, against the will of the Cuban people.

Tell us about the kind of nation that emerged in 1902. Was the U.S. military takeover immediately followed by an economic takeover?

Actually, when the Americans took over militarily in 1902, they had already taken over economically. Americans owned extensive tracts of land in Cuba by the end of the 10-year war. The Spanish landowners, even though they had won the war, were ruined financially and sold their land off cheap to the Americans. So there was a major invasion of U.S. capital, and by the beginning of the century about 70 percent of the land in Cuba was in U.S. hands.

But capitalist development really took off after the war, when more and more U.S. companies came to the island to exploit our natural and human resources. On the positive side, they brought in new technology and new jobs, and Havana quickly developed. But the rural areas and the social needs of the majority were neglected. Out of six million inhabitants, nearly one million were totally illiterate, and more than half a million people were unemployed. Many people at that time migrated to the United States, just as today Mexicans, Dominicans and others leave their poor countries for the wealthier United States.

Another feature of capitalism for us was corruption and repression, which became a daily fact of life. Politics was run by gangsters and gangsterism became part of the private enterprise system in Cuba, with the presence of the international mafia — Meyer Lansky, Lucky Luciano and the rest. Cuba became a paradise for corrupt people, and our tourist industry was geared toward that. Before pornography really existed in the United States, Cuba had a well-developed industry with things like live sex acts on stage.

And of course repression was severe because the country was so ungovernable.

Why was it so ungovernable?

You had a country that had been fighting for its independence through two very cruel and protracted wars, but whose independence was frustrated by an American intervention. We watched our independence fighters be stripped of their dignity and thrown onto unemployment lines, dying in the streets without honor or dignity. We later saw how gangsters ran our country with the new oligarchy. But we also saw that the real power was the United States — in fact, the U.S. ambassador clearly had more power than the Cuban president. At the same time, we had a country with such growing inequalities, which was exactly the opposite of the dream of José Martí.

All this was very frustrating for a country that had a very strong, deep-rooted, nationalistic heritage and egalitarian values. This is what made our society continuously explosive. There were constant strikes, strong working-class unions and the emergence of revolutionary leaders. The tradition of armed struggle against oppression was also a very deep-rooted tradition in Cuba because of the example of the Mambis, who took up arms against Spain. There were armed uprisings in the 1920s, in the 1930s, and again in the 1950s against Batista. So all these factors make Cuba a peculiar nation. If you were a dogmatic Marxist trying to explain the Cuban revolution from purely material conditions, you would have no explanation — this was not the most backward country in Latin America nor the most developed.

The 1959 revolution was supposed to recapture our early goals. It was supposed to give the Cuban people not only their independence as a nation but also a republic "con todos y para el bien de todos," with all and for the good of all, as promised by José Martí.

So the revolution triumphed in 1959, and immediately entered into a collision course with the U.S. government. I remember that Fidel Castro went to the United States early in 1959. He was never received by President Eisenhower, but instead met with then-vice president Nixon. Nixon talked with Fidel for about an hour, and then reported to Eisenhower that Castro was a very dangerous man, and the revolution was also a very dangerous process. What was it about the revolution that the United States found so threatening?

The issue that first brought out the differences between the two countries was our attempt to bring about a more just distribution of land. On May 17, 1959, the new revolutionary government passed an Agrarian Reform Law. The United States was opposed to the law because it included the nationalization of the largest landowners of Cuba, including the U.S. company United Fruit,

now United Brands. The nationalization included the indem-
nification of those lands; it was not intended to be a
nationalization without compensation. Nevertheless the idea of
taking away land from a U.S. company was enough to make the
United States furious.

This land reform was not a socialist reform. In fact, if you
compare it to the Land Reform Law that the United States tried to
implement in El Salvador in the 1980s, ours was in certain aspects
a moderate one. But of course its radicalism was related to the
fact that this was happening over 30 years ago, and it was totally
unacceptable to the United States at the time.

So the Agrarian Reform Law was signed on May 17, 1959,
and just two days later President Eisenhower signed the Pluto
Plan, which aimed to destabilize Cuba. Pluto was the CIA's code
name for the comprehensive program of subversion that cul-
minated in the Bay of Pigs invasion.

**This means that the collision course between the Cuban
revolution and the U.S. government began before Cuba had
declared itself socialist, which occurred during the Bay of Pigs
invasion in 1961, and before Cuba even had relations with the
Soviet Union.**

Precisely. That is why, when people wonder why U.S.-Cuban
tensions have not eased now that the Cold War is over, I reply
that the problems between the United States and Cuba have very
little to do with the Cold War. They have little to do with
communism or socialism or even with the personality of Fidel
Castro. They have more to do with the Monroe Doctrine of the
last century — that the Americas should belong to the United
States — than the Truman Doctrine of containing communism.
They have to do with the fact that since the last century, the
United States has believed it had a manifest destiny to bring its
brand of civilization to the southern part of the hemisphere.

The problem for the Cuban revolution is not so much that it
became a communist revolution but that it proclaimed from the
very beginning that it was going to take an independent path
from that of the United States. The clash that began with the

United States as early as 1959 had less to do with Nixon's or the CIA's assessment that the revolution's leaders were Marxists than with the assessment that that leadership would promote independent policies both within the country and abroad.

You are saying, then, that the socialist nature of the revolution was not determined by the vision of the revolution's leaders but by the reaction of the United States to the revolution's reforms. Others claim the opposite is true. For example, Tad Szulc, in his biography of Fidel, makes a major issue of the fact that a number of key leaders in the revolution were Marxists, intellectually speaking, before the triumph of the revolution, even though they were not formally affiliated with any Communist Party. So according to Szulc, if Fidel Castro, Raúl Castro and Che Guevara were Marxists, then it was inevitable that the revolution would become a socialist one.

But no one asks how the masses turned in favor of socialism, and this is a key question. This country was strongly anti-communist in 1958 and 1959. We were under the total cultural and ideological hegemony of the national and international media at that time, a media that demonized communism.

When the United States began fomenting overt and covert hostility toward Cuba — as early as May 1959 — it unwittingly also began a process of educating the Cuban masses in the socialist alternative. The Cuban people began to see socialism as the only alternative to the kind of society in which they had previously lived and to the kind of relationship they had formerly had with the United States. And they began to see that the only way to resist the aggression of the United States was to radicalize the revolution in order to defeat the United States and its local allies. This included befriending the Soviet Union and Eastern Europe in order to create a relationship of forces that could preserve Cuba's sovereignty.

So thanks to the United States, the Cuban people entered into a very quick and dialectical process of education. That's the only possible explanation of how a group of Marxist intellectual leaders were able to convert an anti-communist people to socialism in the course of a few months.

Trends and stages of a revolution

Did these Marxist intellectual leaders of the Cuban revolution have a unified vision of how to build that revolution? Or were there major differences in the leadership about the path to socialism?

There has been one process, one revolution, but inside that revolution there have coexisted different trends and schools of socialist thinking, different ways of conceiving what kind of socialism we should try to build.

On the one hand, you had the political currents of Che Guevara and Fidel Castro, as leaders attempting to bring about a different brand of socialism than that which already existed in Europe and the Soviet Union. They thought the Cuban model should take into account that Cuba was a Latin American country and not a European one, should take into account the ideals of Martí about building a united but democratic revolutionary party as well as an independent republic with social justice. If you look back at the speeches by Che and Fidel during the 1960s, you will see a consistent attempt to build an alternative socialist model, one that would avoid the mistakes, the traumas, and the gross violations of rights that took place in many of those countries such as Romania and Poland.

On the other hand, we also had revolutionaries who were educated in the Soviet Union or within the context of the theoretical works of the Soviet Union. Some, like my parents, were members of the old Communist Party. They had a certain legitimate admiration for the Soviet Union and believed that the kind of socialism we should foster in Cuba was the same brand which already prevailed in that country and the Eastern bloc.

Why do you call this admiration for the Soviet Union a "legitimate" one?

After all, the Bolshevik revolution accomplished the miracle of transforming a very backward country into a first class power in the world, and a power that had a fairer system of distribution than many developed capitalist countries. And remember it did this while having the monumental task of reconstructing the country twice, once after it was invaded by counterrevolutionaries from 1917-1921, and later on after World War II, when the Soviets defeated the Nazis but paid a high price in both lives and resources.

So how did these two different visions — the Soviet model versus the alternative Latin model — coexist?

These two different ideological conceptions of socialism and of how to construct socialism in Cuba have coexisted and still coexist within our country, both among the leadership and the grassroots level of our population. The difference between our process and, for example, that in China or the Soviet Union or Hungary, is that we have thus far been able to maintain our unity within those two major conceptual trends without eliminating one or the other. Fortunately, in the Cuban case these two schools of thought have not acted or organized as factions within the revolution or the Communist Party. They simply represent two kinds of authentic revolutionaries who share the common goal of building socialism but disagree on how to get there.

One thing we can be very proud of is the way these different visions have managed to coexist peacefully, and Fidel Castro should be given credit for this. Contrast this to what often happened in the Soviet Union, where any time there was a change of direction, half the Central Committee went to prison, faced a firing squad or fell in disgrace. Or look at China, where half the Central Committee was wiped out during the Cultural Revolution. In our case, the two groups have been able to work together, although in various stages, one or the other vision has prevailed. The lesson of 1878 was finally learned by this generation. Divisions make revolutions fail, while pluralism is not only desirable but also a necessity for a revolution's survival.

Can you talk a little more about those different visions and the different stages the revolution has gone through?

In the first stage, during the sixties, it was basically the ideas of Fidel Castro and Che Guevara that prevailed. Che's criticism of the Soviet Union and the socialist camp was that they were obsessed with the economic construction of socialism and that they were disregarding the moral and spiritual factors of socialist societies. Che once said in an interview that he was not interested in economic socialism. If you disregard the spiritual factors and only attempt to deal with economic factors, you are not going to get rid of alienation. For both Che and Fidel, socialism was not simply a matter of developing a new way of distribution. It was a question of freeing people from alienation at the same time.

This was a crucial and very clear distinction between the kind of socialism we wanted to build and that which was already in progress in the Soviet Union and the Eastern bloc at that time.

What made it possible for this alternative vision to prevail during the sixties?

The sixties was a time of questioning and upheaval all over the world, giving us more space for experimentation. There was the Vietnam War and the anti-war movement in the United States. It was the time of student insurrections in places like Berkeley and Paris and the time of the Cultural Revolution in China. It was the time of the Soviet invasion of Czechoslovakia. There were revolutionary struggles being waged throughout Latin America. There was Che Guevara himself and his vision of creating a new person with a new set of values.

The sixties was a time when we attempted to create a totally new way of organizing the economy that would promote solidarity and cooperation between both individuals and economic enterprises instead of competition. It was also a time of discussing freedom — intellectual freedom, individual freedom, the way to secure individuality within the context of a communist society.

You speak with great nostalgia about the sixties.

It was a crucial time for our revolution and for the world as well.
I think one of the things we should all do one day is to sit and
discuss the sixties and what it all meant — especially as we
approach the closing of the century.

**Yet you say that the vision of the sixties, even in Cuba, lost out.
What happened?**

Several things happened to derail this vision. On the one hand,
there were internal factors. The Cuban economy became mis-
managed after Guevara left Cuba in 1965 for the internationalist
mission that he was committed to. His ideas were not discarded
after he left, but many of them were actually pushed too fast after
his departure. This brought about a degree of mismanagement of
the economy that produced a critical situation for Cuba at the end
of the sixties.

**Could you explain that? What do you mean when you say that
his ideas were pushed too fast?**

For example, a campaign to reduce bureaucracy — a valid idea —
turned into the destruction of the accounting system that Che had
left behind. Without accurate and reliable data, no capitalist
enterprise could operate, and this lack of data was even more
devastating for a socialist centralized economy.

Another issue is that of material versus moral incentives. Che
believed that social consciousness should become the main
motivation for production, but after his departure this idea was
really carried out by decree and not by long-term policies. It is
one thing to try little by little to plant the seed of the new
consciousness within the population by education and another to
say that starting tomorrow there will be no more extra pay in the
factory and everybody will work on the basis of moral incentives.
And that's basically what happened. We pushed too fast and the
people were not ready for it.

What about the 1968 "ofensiva revolucionaria," the revolutionary offensive that banned all private selling? Isn't this another example of pushing too fast? Instead of trying to eliminate the worst excesses of the marketplace, the government eliminated the market itself.

Exactly. In 1968 we wiped out private enterprise, from the woman running a hamburger stand to the guy selling snow cones on the street corner. It was again done by decree, forbidding people from entering into market relations, rather than through a slower process of both educating the population and setting up an alternative to replace the vacuum created by this loss of private enterprise.

I think there was a valid concern that market relations should not run the society, that the society should be run on a more humane basis to guarantee the basics to everyone. I understand the nationalization of the nation's major industries. But in terms of small businesses, I think that instead of eliminating them they could have been regulated in their transactions, making sure that market relations did not become the general trend of the economy. By pushing them aside in one fell swoop, the Cuban economy never recovered from that blow. Goods became scarce, inflation resulted because people had a lot of money and not much to buy, and the problem of poor services continues to haunt us today.

Another economic disaster in the late 1960s was the push for the 10-million ton sugar harvest. This self-imposed goal of producing 10-million tons of sugar in 1969-1970 was designed to take advantage of the relatively high price of sugar in the international market at that time and to get Cuba enough money to launch a major development program. The goal was not only too ambitious (representing about 3 million tons more than Cuba had ever produced) and was not achieved, but it also produced tremendous dislocations in the rest of the economy. This all-out drive for sugar meant that other sectors of the economy, including food production, were neglected. This failure must have been a major factor in the reassessment of the

socialist path Cuba had been following.

Yes, it certainly was a major setback. But in addition to these internal factors we've been discussing, there were also a number of international setbacks that forced us to realign our policies. Guevara's death and the defeat of the guerrillas in many parts of Latin America at the end of the sixties left Cuba more isolated. In Vietnam, the replacement of U.S. troops by South Vietnamese troops and by more intensive bombing allowed the United States to end the draft, which led to a demobilization of the anti-war movement in the United States and allowed Washington to focus more on other foreign policy "problems" like Cuba. In general, the more conservative atmosphere that followed the 1960s unrest in many parts of the world was not beneficial to the Cuban process.

So with an international environment that was not exactly supportive of the Cuban revolution, we were obliged to reassess both the situation and the perspectives of the Cuban revolution. During that debate, which took place in the early 1970s, it was said that the only possibility of defending Cuba in that adverse environment was to strengthen our alliance with the Soviet Union and Eastern Europe. And with this alliance, throughout the 1970s and the first half of the 1980s, little by little we began to import the Soviet model of socialism into different areas of the Cuban society.

You say you were forced to strengthen your alliance with the Soviet bloc. Relations with the Soviets must have been quite poor after the 1962 Missile Crisis, when Cuba was angry with the Soviets for having negotiated with the United States for a solution to the crisis behind Cuba's back.

Cuban-Soviet relations suffered after the Missile Crisis, but improved afterwards when Fidel went to the Soviet Union and spoke to Khrushchev. But this rapprochement was affected by the radical policies Cuba was following internationally, its support for the guerrilla movements in Latin America and in Africa.

Against the will of the Soviets?

Against the wisdom of the Soviets. And internally, our notions about constructing socialism in a different way were creating tensions in the relationship. The worst years were 1964-1967. I remember in 1967 when Premier Kosygin came to Cuba the relations were as cold as could be.

But by the early 1970s, the Cuban revolution was in trouble both because of internal economic problems and a less hospitable international climate, and those who favored closer ties with the Soviets won out. Can you describe this second phase of the revolution, and what elements of the Soviet model were incorporated into the Cuban system?

This second stage of the revolution was characterized not so much by creativity or imagination or the search for a unique Cuban identity but by the political and economic institutionalization of the Cuban revolution under the increasing influence of the Soviet model. Sure, we made adjustments to our reality and came out with some unique institutions such as our legislative body, called People's Power. But basically we copied the essential elements of the Soviet model in its overall conception of the economy, its relationship with politics and the pervasive view of dogmatic Marxism as universal truths. We also created an unnecessary overdependence on the Soviet Union that was not healthy.

In our economy, we copied an absurd model that was based on a stupid, theoretical concept of creating "values" and on fulfilling your yearly plan to create these values, instead of actually creating useful goods. Let's say that you were the head of a construction company and you were told by the government that this year you had to create values of three million pesos. Fine. They didn't say that you had to construct three bridges and two schools, they said you had to create values of three million pesos. Their concept of creating values was spending that amount in labor and resources. So you could create three million pesos in values by moving land, digging ditches, putting in some columns here and there, but having nothing finished or useful in the end.

It's like in the Soviet Union where they were measuring the productivity of a chair factory not by the number of chairs it made, or how comfortable those chairs were, or how cost-effective they were in producing them, but by the total weight of the chairs. So you go to the Soviet Union and you need a crane to carry a chair, because they would make furniture as heavy as possible to "overfulfill" their yearly plan.

One of the funniest things in Cuba is that you could be driving along a highway and see a bridge built up on one side and on the other side, but nothing connecting them.

And the construction group that did it probably successfully completed its plan.

Oh yes, they probably overfulfilled their plan. They probably even got an award for being good workers, for creating a lot of "value."

Another irony of this Soviet model is that it disregarded social needs. Under this system, things such as childcare centers, schools and hospitals — social services in general — were listed as unproductive expenditures and the orientation was to spend in productive areas. So construction for social needs was disregarded and we were accumulating more and more social problems in terms of lack of housing, childcare centers, schools, hospitals, etc.

Another problem we found is that unlike the focus on moral incentives in the 1960s, material incentives had become the motivating force for workers. Not only were people losing the sense of working for the common good, but these material incentives usually had little to do with the final outcome of their work. So people were making a lot of money, but not producing more or more efficiently.

Didn't this mentality of divorcing the work from the final results also affect the education system? I remember during this time that the teachers' main interest was promoting all the students so they could reach their yearly promotion goals. The quality of education suffered because students who should have been left behind were promoted to reach these abstract goals.

Yes, with this Soviet model, quality and concrete results suffered. So this kind of madness existed throughout our system, and after some 15 years it became obvious that something was very wrong.

In fact, I would say that the worst error we committed, the one with the most dramatic and lasting effects, was the decision to follow the Soviet model of socialism. Those 15 years of "Russification" of our socialism left us with problems in almost every realm of Cuban society.

In the economy, it introduced the notion of state socialism and vertical command based on a primitive and incompetent style of authoritarian central planning. In politics, it promoted the bureaucratization of organizations that were once full of creativity and initiative by transforming them into formal extensions of the Party machinery, while restricting the limits of pluralism in society as a whole. Socially, an attempt to legitimize special privileges for a new managerial bureacratic strata negatively affected the revolutionary spirit of our process. Culturally, it certainly killed the possibility of using social science — and Marxism for that matter — as a useful tool in the consturction of the new society when they were transformed into a religious creed for the apologetic praising of official policies.

Several generations of cadre and professors were inculcated with this adulterated and manipulative version of socialism. The rectification campaign was launched in the mid-1980s to overcome some of these problems that were perverting our process.

This third stage of the Cuban revolution, what you call the rectification process, was talked about in Cuba as Cuba's own form of "perestroika." It took place years before the Soviet Union began its reform process and involved "delinking" from the Soviet model. Did Cuba begin to decouple itself from the Soviet bloc solely because you were looking at problems within Cuba itself, or were you also looking at problems within the Soviet Union when you began the rectification campaign?

We did not attempt to wean ourselves economically from the Soviet sphere. We were instead concerned that the Eastern European model was not a good model for constructing socialism in Cuba. We distanced ourselves from the idea that what worked for the Soviets would necessarily work for the Cubans, and yes, we also started to realize that this model was not even working that well for the Soviets. I think Fidel himself had the wisdom of seeing what was going to happen in the Soviet bloc before it started. Remember, he launched the rectification process well before perestroika even existed.

When was that?

Officially speaking, the rectification process in Cuba began in April 1986 when Fidel Castro gave a speech calling for a revamping of many of our economic and political policies. But this process really started in 1984 after the U.S. invasion of Grenada, and it started in the military field with a reassessment of the defense doctrine of Cuba.

What happened in Grenada to cause this reassessment? Did the fact that the United States invaded Grenada make Cuba more concerned about a direct invasion? I remember that Alexander Haig, who was Reagan's secretary of state at the time, was making hostile statements about going to the source of revolutionary upheaval in the region, by which he meant Cuba.

Yes, and it was not only the invasion of Grenada that concerned us. The United States was also seriously considering intervening in El Salvador and Nicaragua. So we had to take the threat of a possible invasion very seriously.

In this process of reexamining our defense system, we reached the conclusion that we had wrongly copied the defense model of the Soviet Union and the Eastern bloc of relying on a regular army, which is only a small segment of the population. We decided to revise that approach, going back to our earlier notions of the 1960's when we thought that the defense of the Cuban revolution should be the task of the entire population.

As a result, some three million people were organized and trained in martial arts or tasks related to defense. In those years, the Reagan years, we tripled our imports of military hardware to arm this new force. We distributed weapons in factories, farms, universities, different neighborhoods in cities and small towns throughout the island to make sure that the population would have immediate access to them in case of a U.S. invasion.

This was a very serious step not only militarily speaking, but also politically and philosophically. Because when you arm the population, you have to make sure that you have the consensus of the population. It is the acid test for any government. When you rely upon a professional army, you have that army under your control. But when you're giving weapons to students and factory workers, when you're creating arsenals in remote places in the mountains, when you're giving both access to and control of those weapons to the entire population, you have to be absolutely sure that most of the population is backing up your policies.

No other government in Latin America would feel secure enough to arm the population, as we did in Cuba. I have spent quite a lot of time in Bolivia. I am sure that no Bolivian government — nor Argentine, Brazilian, or Dominican government — would be willing to give arms to its people. Look at Venezuela, which has had democratically-elected governments but has been wracked by social explosions. It would have been suicidal for former President Carlos Andres Pérez to train university students and workers in military exercises and give them weapons. It would probably have resulted in a civil war for radical social change.

Reducing the role of defense to professional armies was, after all, part of the general model of domination imposed by the United States on the countries of Latin America. Reducing the role of the defense of popular processes to professional armies and police is partially responsible for the failure of socialism in Eastern Europe and the Soviet Union, for it allowed their governments and parties to distance themselves from the people.

So I think that this 1984 reassessment of our defense system was historically very important. It re-activated our original concept of the importance of the people's participation in defending their revolution and stressed our vision of an "armed democracy" as evidence of respect for Cuba's sovereignty.

How did rectification play out in the economy?

After reshaping the island's system of defense, we entered a process of reassessing our economic policies. First, we scrutinized our strategy of development and, second, the manner in which our economy had been structured according to the Soviet model.

For example, we decided to change our concept of state planning, to make sure that planning did not mean — as it used to — a total centralization of decision-making at all levels. We were trying to strike a balance between centralized and decentralized decisions in a planned economy and to debureaucratize our planning process.

This is also the time that we geared our development to high technology. This had long been a Cuban position which had always clashed with that of the CMEA [the Council for Mutual Economic Assistance], the socialist trading bloc. A number of countries within that bloc tried to impose a traditional international division of labor that mimicked the division of labor in the capitalist world, with Cuba and other Third World socialist countries producing raw commodities and the more industrialized socialist countries producing manufactured goods.

When we said we wanted to develop a high-tech industry in Cuba, they said "Why? That's the role of East Germany, that's the role of Bulgaria. You have to take care of supplying nickel and sugar and other traditional exports. That's your natural competitive advantage." We had a long debate and many discussions, but we insisted on changing this traditional view and finally Cuba was accepted as part of the long-term CMEA project, for example, to develop computers.

As early as the 1960s, Che Guevara and Fidel Castro had pointed out that the only way to achieve true development in the second half of the 20th century was through the mastery of some aspect of high technology. I remember that even back then, Che used Japan as an example, saying Japan is an island that doesn't even have fertile land. It's mostly rocks. It lacks oil and has very few raw materials. The basic wealth of Japan is the talent and education of the Japanese people and their capacity to import raw materials, transform them into industrial goods with aggregated value, and export them again.

Starting around 1982, we began to invest heavily in biotechnology, as well as other high-tech areas. By the end of the 1980s, we had already invested the equivalent of several billion dollars in these areas. The three key areas we have been developing are biotechnology, pharmaceuticals, and computerized medical equipment and software.

How did the rectification process address this long-standing controversy of material versus moral incentives?

As part of this process we began to rectify the essence of the economic mechanisms we had been using. We realized that we could not develop an alternative society based on solidarity and feelings of love for your neighbor while using capitalist economic incentives, which foster a dog-eat-dog mentality. So we recaptured the use of moral incentives, which had been set aside for nearly 15 years. We did not discard material incentives, we understood that material incentives were also important to motivate people. But little by little we began to recover the idea that the revolution was not only a matter of a more just distribution of wealth, but also a spiritual project to release people's creativity and give them a greater degree of participation in society.

One of the issues that came up in this rectification campaign was the issue of corruption. Throughout the revolution's history there has been a flourishing black market where people sell goods stolen from state enterprises or hoard scarce goods and resell them. Rectification not only highlighted these problems of corruption among private citizens but also corruption among high government officials.

Yes. Once we began the rectification process, we realized that there were top and middle-level figures — ministers and others — who had become corrupt during this period when we were copying the Eastern institutions. So a number of government officials were charged and tried for corruption.

When we faced this reality of corruption, we also had to look into another, more disagreeable reality, and that is that people are not born corrupt, they get corrupted. They were revolutionaries before but had gone through a process of corruption, because our own institutions had allowed them to go through that process. We were shocked by this. We realized that our system failed to prevent this level of corruption because it did not provide for sufficient popular control.

This really hit home in 1989, when we discovered that a number of important officials of the Army and the Ministry of the Interior were involved in drug smuggling. One of them, General Ochoa, was a hero of the revolution. Of course, he lost that position when we learned that he was connected with drug dealers. To a certain degree, this was precisely the reverse of what happened with Oliver North in the United States, when it was learned that he had all these dealings with the Contras and drug dealers. Oliver North became a celebrity; Ochoa faced a firing squad.

Of course, you know that in the Western press the drug scandal with Ochoa was portrayed as a coverup for a power play between Ochoa and Raúl Castro. Is there any merit to that interpretation?

I really don't think so. I knew Ochoa, and he was not a man who was out for political power. I think this power struggle idea was a media concoction to sow division where it didn't exist.

Getting back to rectification, what effect did it have on the political system?

Rectification led us to a careful review of our political system, with a serious search for ways to get people more involved in the political process. In early 1991 we opened a national discussion with an open agenda in every single workplace, school, university and neighborhood, so that people could openly and freely discuss the problems of Cuban society and how they felt those problems should be dealt with. Their criticisms and suggestions were actively solicited. During the several months of this nationwide discussion, more than a million opinions, criticisms and proposals were recorded.

All these contributions were processed and circulated to delegates of the Communist Party Congress, who also were elected in a more democratic manner than ever before. For the first time there were direct delegates proposed by the rank and file party membership rather than a list of possible candidates presented to the rank and file for voting. This time people were selected by their peers to attend the congress.

The Fourth Party Congress in 1991 was also a peculiar congress if you compare it with any of those previously held. It was a very open, democratic discussion. Normally, the party congress — this was the tradition in the Soviet Union and the Eastern bloc — is opened by the first secretary of the Communist Party (in this case Fidel), who gives his assessment of everything that happened during the past five years. Typically, he also presents his ideas as to how the congress should proceed. Fidel decided that he was not going to do that, because he didn't want to preempt the discussion. He simply made some opening remarks on the current situation we were facing, and then opened the floor for debate.

For those who have a picture of the Cuban revolution from the outside, especially as it is portrayed in the international media, the notion of democracy within the Cuban party is a very difficult one to accept. They think that a one-party system, *per se*, precludes the possibility of democracy. Moreover, they think that Fidel Castro decides the outcome of every issue the country faces. But this just isn't so.

During the second stage of the revolution, from the 1970s to the first half of the 1980s, Fidel Castro's views on more than one issue represented, in fact, a minority within the party and he has acknowledged that he was overruled on several political and economic issues. He has always accepted the majority opinion, even if he disagreed with it.

That's not new. During the fight against Batista he also had this style of accepting collective decisions. For instance, he never thought that the idea of calling for a general strike against Batista in April 1958 was a sound one, but he accepted it because it was the criteria of the majority. The strike was a disaster and the very existence of the revolution was put in jeopardy.

Fidel sometimes criticized what was going on in the 1970s — I remember one speech in which he said that some things in this revolution were legal but they were not moral. But he didn't try to impose his will because he knew that democracy and unity were more precious for us than imposing a view even if it was a correct one.

So how did Fidel manage to start the rectification campaign? What was happening in the mid-1980s that allowed his view to prevail?

It had become obvious to many people at that time that the model of development that we imported from the Soviet Union had begun to reach the point of stagnation. Therefore, it was easier for Fidel Castro and those who sympathized with his point of view to present the problems we were facing and to propose a re-examination of our own roots in an effort to put our socialist process back on a more authentic path.

The fall of the Soviet Union and the "special period"

What happened to the rectification process once Cuba was hit by the severe economic crisis caused by the break-up of the Soviet bloc in 1989? In fact, Cuba's economy was so hard hit that in 1991 the government proclaimed the "special period," which is a euphemism for saying that the economy is really on a wartime footing although there is technically no war.

It must be virtually impossible to think about overhauling political and economic systems when you are dealing with immediate, day-to-day crises.

Cuba is presently going through two parallel crises. One is

structural, arising from our copying of the Soviet model. We had started to seriously address this structural crisis through the rectification campaign when we were affected by a conjunctural crisis that began in 1989 with the upheavals in the Soviet Union.

The dissolution of the Soviet Union and the socialist bloc meant that overnight over 85 percent of our markets disappeared. To make matters worse, the Bush administration, knowing that the upheavals in Soviet Union would cause a crisis in the Cuban economy, tightened the blockade to squeeze Cuba even harder.

So we are certainly in a deep crisis, but first let me explain what I mean by that word. When I use the word crisis, I'm not talking about it the way Western journalists often do, implying a kind of apocalypse. If you look up the word crisis in the dictionary, it has a medical definition. It marks the turning point in the course of a disease, which, yes, can lead to death, but it can also lead to recovery. I use the term the way doctors use it when you have to make some radical reform of your system in order to survive. If you have an appendicitis, you have to first understand that you have the condition, and then take measures to deal with it. If you don't take the correct measures in time, you may die. But if you do take correct measures, the crisis does not have to be lethal.

We in Cuba are aware of the need for change. We know that we are in a critical moment that presents a danger to our system. This means we must lead the crisis and not let the crisis lead us. We have been criticizing the Soviet model of socialism, but we have not yet come up with an alternative. We are inevitably moving towards a mixed economy in terms of the relations of production and we are trying to save the socialist nature of the redistribution of wealth created through this mixed economy.

Do you think this is possible?

This is a very difficult, a very tricky task with no certain outcome. When you are a revolutionary you can't go to Lloyds of London and ask for an insurance policy to insure the success of your revolution. There are no guarantees in this business. But I think we should be given credit for trying to come up with an alternative socialist model during such difficult times.

I remember when I was first studying Marxism, I was intrigued with the discussions about whether it was possible to construct socialism in one country — and here we are trying to construct socialism in one small island surrounded by a capitalist sea! We may not achieve the complete construction of an authentic socialist society in the current circumstances — I don't think that's really possible. But if we are able to keep the revolution alive and moving in that direction despite the present adversities, I think we will have been extremely successful. If we try and fail, the world should at least give us credit for the dignity and heroism of our attempt.

Can you give us a few figures so that we can grasp the extent of Cuba's crisis?

The figures are dramatic. In 1989 we imported about 13 million tons of oil from the Soviet Union; in 1992 we could only import 6 million tons. In 1989 we imported around $8.4 billion worth of goods; by 1992 our import capacity plunged to $2.2 billion. By 1992 we had only 30 percent of the resources for the sugar harvest that we had in 1989, so sugar production was the lowest in 30 years.

When we lost the trade with the socialist bloc, not only did we lose our markets, but we lost a kind of trade in which our prices were indexed to those of our trading partners. For example, if the price of oil went up, the price of sugar would go up as well, and the reverse was also true. At the beginning of the revolution, the international prices of oil and sugar were different than they are today. In those days, with around one million tons of sugar you could buy about eight million tons of oil in the world market. But today we can only get 1.4 million tons of oil for that same one million tons of sugar.

So Cuba was in trouble once it lost the subsidized trade relations it had with the Soviet Union.

For several years the fair terms of trade we had with the Soviet

Union with indexed prices were the essence of what the Nonaligned Movement and the Third World in general demanded from the West at the United Nations. What the Western countries called a subsidy of Cuba by the Soviet Union was in reality fair trade terms between a developed and a developing country. But of course that is unthinkable for the West. It was then and it is even more unthinkable today.

So when we lost those terms of trade, as well as our markets and sources of technology, our economy was devastated. Imagine what would happen to Mexico if suddenly all trade with the United States ceased? And when they tried to find new markets, new sources of technology, a superpower would be there to stop them from finding these new outlets. Mexicans would not be able to buy the goods they have become so dependent on. They would suddenly lose the markets for the vast majority of their products. They would be cut off from all credit, investment, and technology.

I don't know how the Mexican government could handle such a shock to the economy and still keep the people behind it. There would probably be great political upheaval. But that economic scenario is what happened to Cubans almost overnight when we learned in late December 1991 that the Soviet Union was gone!

Does Cuba still have trade relations with the Russian republics?

We still have relationships with Russia and the various republics, but there are several problems. We don't trade in as many products as we did before and we don't have the same terms of trade.

Again, with the Soviet Union we achieved what was supposed to be the New International Economic Order for the Third World. This protected us from the fluctuations of the market and that gave us the possibility of planning ahead — 5 years, 10 years — with a more or less stable income. We have lost that.

Not only have we lost the indexing, but we don't know from one year to the next how much they are going to buy from us and how much they have to sell. The prices now fluctuate

according to the international market. So there is great
uncertainty. A number of products they used to sell to us have
disappeared or are being redirected to Western markets.

For example, they sold us different brands of cars, like Lada
or Moscovich. Ladas are still being produced, but they are now
being sold on the Western markets. So it's hard for us to even get
spare parts now. And they are changing the models and are not
very interested in producing spare parts for the old models. The
other brand, Moscovich, was discontinued because it was not
profitable according to Western standards. Whoever has one of
those cars in Cuba has a big problem because it is impossible to
get spare parts. So there are numerous problems in this
relationship, many of which stem from internal uncertainties
within the Russian republics.

**Can you describe how this economic crisis affects the daily lives
of ordinary Cubans?**

It means hardship for every single Cuban. The food supply of the
population has been dramatically affected, because much of our
foods and animal feed was imported from the Eastern bloc. The
average Cuban today is getting around one-third of the consumer
goods — food, clothing, etc. — that he or she received in 1989,
although the social services like health care remain in place.

Then there's another complicating factor. Just when we
thought we had reached rock bottom, we were hit by a terrible
storm in March 1993 that was the worst storm in the century. It
did over one billion dollars worth of damage. Remember, this was
in an economy that in 1992 had an import capacity of only $2.2
billion. The storm destroyed over 40,000 homes. It destroyed a
large portion of the crops in the greenbelt surrounding Havana.
And many hotels, which bring Cuba much-needed hard currency,
were severely damaged.

For the first time in the 35 years of the revolution, we had to
go to the international community for emergency relief. Some U.S.
non-governmental organizations asked their government to make
a humanitarian gesture of excluding food and medicines from the
embargo, but to no avail.

You should know that for the past 30 years, Cuba has been helping others during times of crisis without regard to ideology. We offered help to Somoza in Nicaragua after the devastating earthquake, we gave help to the Salvadorans under Duarte, we also offered help — which was not accepted — to the United States after Hurricane Andrew. So now when it was our turn to expect some human sensitivity during our crisis, the United States remained aloof.

For the past few decades, Cuba has had a low per capita GNP but a high standard of living in comparison to other Third World countries. With this present crisis, how would you compare Cuba today to the rest of Latin America?

The crisis we are going through in Cuba is very real and very profound, but it is also relative. If you would bring a working-class Bolivian to Cuba, they would think this was paradise. The same with poor people from Venezuela, or Mexico, or the Dominican Republic, or Honduras. There are 60 million people in northeast Brazil who are living in conditions that are much worse than any of the 11 million Cubans live with.

In the middle of this disastrous economic period, we still run all of our social services free. We might have to close factories for lack of spare parts or fuel, but workers go home with 60 percent of their salary guaranteed. If you are sick, you will never be fired from your job; you will be maintained by the state, free of charge, and in many cases with 100 percent of your salary. So our crisis is certainly not at the level of Somalia or Ethiopia, and not at the level of many places in Latin America either.

But the Cuban population was accustomed to a certain standard of living, it was used to having a number of social benefits in health and education that people in the United States don't even have. These services have deteriorated as a result of the crisis in the 1990s, and life is much, much more difficult than it was just five years ago.

One of the most serious complaints Cubans have is about the lack of food. How are you dealing with the need to quickly

increase the volume of food at a time when there is no money to buy fertilizers and pesticides, and there is almost no fuel to run the tractors or the bring the food to market?

We have a crash program for food production, but it will be impossible to be self-sustaining until we are a couple of years down the road. While this lack of fertilizers and pesticides might prove beneficial over the long term by forcing us to develop biological controls, for now it poses a tremendous challenge.

One of the key aspects we are relying on for producing more food quickly is agricultural brigades, which are based on volunteer work from people in the cities. The major cities require a lot of labor in the agricultural belts that surround them. At a time when we have no material rewards to offer people to do the hard work involved in food production, these volunteer brigades are crucial for our survival. In these moments you see how right Che Guevara was when he said that the Cuban society must rely basically on moral incentives because we could never compete with the consumer society up north. If we had trained our people to expect solely material incentives, in this critical moment we would have never been able to do what we did in 1992 — mobilize 150,000 people from the city to work in the countryside for 15 days or one month at a time. This political education is the only thing that is making the revolution viable in this time of crisis.

Another help in coping with this severe crisis in agriculture is the capacity of our scientists to use advances in biotechnology and organic agriculture to come up with ecological controls as alternatives to imported fertilizers and pesticides. Had we not, over the years, put this emphasis on the scientific training of our population, we would be in much worse shape today.

Some observers say that Cuba should finally abandon its emphasis on sugar, a commodity that fetches a low price on the international market and takes away from efforts to increase production for local consumption. What is your opinion?

By selling sugar in the international market we receive hard currency to keep the economy running — not only importing the food we need, but also maintaining the education system, the health care system, and other social services.

Sugar has been paying for the majority of our imports. We are also very competitive in sugar production. Many of our sugar mills generate their own fuel from the sugar byproducts, and we use the byproducts for making everything from animal feed to medicines to furniture. So to suddenly break down the sugar economy and enter into another area would not be a wise move. And we still have enough land to plant with food crops.

The real Achilles heal of the Cuban economy is fuel, given Cuba's lack of significant internal fuel sources. I know that Cuba has been increasing its oil production from about 700,000 tons of oil a year in 1988 to about 1.5 million tons in 1992. But this is still a fraction of what is needed, given that in 1989 Cuba was importing some 13 million tons of petroleum from the Soviet Union. What are the chances that a major oil supply may be discovered in Cuba?

There has been oil drilling going on for years now, but as you say our domestic production only represents a fraction of our needs. To increase production, we have had to look for outside capital because offshore drilling is an expensive and risky investment. We are now working with several companies, primarily Canadian and French. They bring the capital and technology; if they don't find any oil, it's their loss. If they do, we share 50 percent of the production. That's the only way we can bring in the capital we need.

Before the collapse of the Soviet Union, the Soviets spent hundreds of millions of dollars helping Cuba build a nuclear power plant. What has happened to this plant?

Remember that the Cuban government did not get involved in this nuclear plant simply because it thought of it as an energy option, but because we had no choice. We don't have our own oil supply, and our geopolitical situation — only 90 miles from the

United States — makes us vulnerable to a naval or air quarantine, as was the case during the Missile Crisis in 1962. So the plant would have given us some energy to keep the essentials going in case of a quarantine. Right now construction on the plant has stopped, because we don't have the resources to keep building it and the Russians haven't extended us credit to do so.

It seems that one of the areas that Cuba is banking on for the future of its economy is its high-tech industry. Can you talk about Cuba's advances in high-tech areas and what impact these sectors might have on the economy?

In the long term, we have been betting on high-tech in biological and pharmaceutical products as the way out for our economy. In entering the next century, the only way that any country can be competitive is by dominating at least one area of high-tech, because it's the area that has more aggregated value than any other.

We have some products that are already being produced by the big pharmaceutical companies, but we also have products that represent real breakthroughs, such as vaccines for hepatitis-B and meningitis-B. I know that there was an outbreak of meningitis in the United States in 1993, and our vaccine could save U.S. lives. So you see the blockade cuts both ways. Not only Cuban but American lives are punished by this insanity.

We have a new kind of recombinant streptokinasis that dissolves blood clots; we have a product called epidermal growth factor for burns. In agriculture we have developed a pill that you put in milk and it keeps the milk from curdling. It allows you to preserve milk without refrigeration, which could be of great benefit for the Third World.

We have a new product for high cholesterol, called PPG, that decreases cholesterol levels and cleanses the arteries. Ateromixol is its clinical name, and it is so safe it can be sold without a doctor's prescription. We have carefully tested PPG, and found that it has only one side effect — it increases sexual activity. But as you can imagine, no one is complaining about this secondary affect. There are foreigners who come here and buy massive amounts thinking it's an aphrodisiac, but it isn't. It is simply that when you have better blood circulation, all the functions of the body, including sexual activity, function better. That's the secret.

So our future in biotechnology, pharmaceuticals, robotics and software is very promising. Of course, it takes a lot of investment. One Japanese microscope can cost $5 million, and you might need two or three in a lab. But the aggregated value that you achieve in the market makes these products very profitable, and our investments are paying off. We have sold about $120 million of the meningitis-B vaccine to Brazil. It is little known in the West that we have even sold some computer software to Japan, which as you know is a very difficult market to enter without a high-quality product.

Are Cuban biotech products competitive in the international market? And isn't Cuba's biggest limitation that it doesn't have the huge sums of money needed to market these products?

Cuba is highly competitive, because our costs are so much lower than in the industrialized countries. For example, there are only four factories in the world that produce monoclonal antibodies — these are in the United States, Germany, Great Britain, and Cuba. We can produce many of them at one-quarter the cost of production in the other plants. This is why some of the major pharmaceutical companies are interested in our biotechnology industry. It has nothing to do with sympathy for the Cuban revolution; it is strictly good business sense.

Our scientists don't drive BMWs, they ride to work in bicycles. They earn salaries of about $300 a month, a fraction of what top scientists are paid elsewhere.

The other aspect is that the prices the drug companies charge for their products often bear no relationship to the cost of production. They can charge 500 times the real costs, because they have monopoly control over the market. We in Cuba could sell our products at a much lower cost and still make plenty of money.

But yes, our biggest limitation is in the marketing of our products. The large international pharmaceutical companies —

there are seven or eight of them — keep other companies out. They do this through a variety of means. For example, they are in favor of protecting their domestic markets, so they work with the state to set all these restrictions on outside companies. Products take years to register and must go through a barrage of clinical tests. All this can take 4-5 years, enough time for the local company to make the same product. This is part of the commercial war that we are dealing with.

So our strategy is not to give priority to the markets of the industrialized nations, but to sell first in Third World markets, where the transnationals have less of a stranglehold. Many Latin American countries, for example, are not currently serviced by the big drug companies because the companies can't make the kind of profits they can make elsewhere.

While high-tech may be the way out in the future, in the short term Cuba needs immediate infusions of cash — and the strategy for that is the tourist industry. Tourism is booming in Cuba now — with about 400,000 tourists visiting the island in 1992. But unlike high-tech, the tourist industry has a number of negative impacts on the internal dynamics of the country. Until August 1993, when it became legal for Cubans to possess U.S. dollars, Cubans were not allowed to use the tourist restaurants and hotels, creating a lot of resentment among Cubans. Prostitution, the scourge of Cuba before the revolution, has returned with tourism. The black market in dollars is rampant. Could you talk about the tourist industry in Cuba, including some of these negative aspects?

Yes, tourism brings with it a lot of problems, but it is also absolutely necessary for our economy right now. On the positive side, tourism is a sector that attracts foreign investors for building hotels, restaurants, nightclubs. We have dozens of joint ventures in tourism with investors from countries such as Canada, Spain, Italy, and Brazil.

It's a sector that is doubling its income every year. Of each dollar, about half needs to be spent on importing goods for the tourist, the rest is profit. In the case of joint ventures, of course, this profit must be shared with the foreign investor.

Cuba's capacity for increasing tourism is great. We have miles and miles of clean beaches and uncontaminated water. We have a healthier atmosphere than many other tourist spots in the Caribbean, with no drugs and almost no violent crime.

I remember hearing an interview a few years ago with the president of the Dominican Republic, Balaguer, and he was asked if he would like to see Fidel Castro gone. "Oh no," he said, "that would ruin us, because all the American tourists would then go to Cuba when the embargo is lifted."

While there are certainly negative consequences of opening up our culture to outsiders, there are also positive consequences. It allows us to appreciate and build on the best of our own culture, and it also can be enriching to be influenced by the diversity of other cultures.

But there are very serious negative aspects to tourism. In general, I see the development of the tourist industry at this time as a kind of chemotherapy for the economy. When you have a cancer, sometimes the only option that you have available is to go through chemotherapy. And as we all know, chemotherapy has such terrible side-effects that it can even kill you before you die from the cancer. Well, the Cuban economy at this moment has a cancer, and we have to take radical decisions in order to keep it afloat. We need to keep the economy afloat because we want to maintain the free educational system, the health care system, food security, the social security system. And to keep all that running, you need to get as much hard currency as possible, in the shortest possible time.

The only industry that can provide that kind of hard currency, in the short term, is tourism. Now the tourist industry has, of course, some negative side effects, as it does in virtually every society where it develops. These include prostitution, increased crime, and black marketing. They are certainly not as significant as in other societies where these areas become the private industry of organized crime and in many cases, go unchecked by the corrupted authorities. But we are nevertheless concerned about this because as the tourist industry grows, so might these social problems.

I'm sure you've heard the term "tourism apartheid", referring to Cuba's system of making tourist facilities off limits to Cubans. Before the legalization of the dollar, Cubans were not allowed to use most of the nation's tourist facilities. Now these facilities are open to Cubans with access to dollars, but this represents only a small portion of the population. The fact remains that most Cubans are barred from many of the country's hotels, restaurants, and night clubs.

I think I first read the term tourism apartheid in the *Miami Herald*. I hate the association of such a reprehensible term — apartheid — with tourism in Cuba, and I don't think it's fair.

Before the revolution we had an apartheid system. When I was a kid, I used to be a member of a humble beach club. Near this club was a rich club for the aristocrats. I remember that I would swim from my club to theirs, but there would be a sailor waiting to kick me out. I could not swim in their water. One of the things the revolution did was to make all the beaches open to everyone. They remain open, as do the doors and halls of the hotels on those beaches, but not every service in those hotels remains open anymore.

If you want to play games with words, I'd say the American system is an apartheid economy. I lived in New York and I knew plenty of people who never imagined visiting the Waldorf Astoria or the World Trade Center. It was off limits to them because of their income.

In Cuba, everyone has equal access to the most basic necessities of life — food, health care, education. Now, in order to maintain this system of equality during a time of economic crisis, we have had to develop our tourism industry. This industry implies a cost in terms of hard currency. As I said, for every dollar we earn, half of it is spent on imported goods for the tourists. If we opened up our tourist facilities to all Cubans, we would not make the hard currency we need to make for our imports. If we rented all the hotels in pesos instead of dollars, Cubans would saturate all the hotels and restaurants.

Denying access to facilities creates an ideological and political problem because the Cuban population has been trained in an egalitarian system by the revolution itself. Since the revolution, every single Cuban correctly believes that he or she has the right to go anywhere in Cuba and have access to any facility. Not only did they have this belief, but they exercised it. Up until this crisis in the late 1980s, almost all facilities used to be open to everyone, and Cubans had plenty of money to spend on "non-essentials" since their basic needs were either free or inexpensive.

So we are sacrificing equality in one area in order to have enough money to maintain equality in other areas. That's why I call it chemotherapy. It's a difficult tradeoff. Hopefully, when we overcome this critical economic situation, we will go back to having equal access to all these facilities, too.

This brings up another controversial policy in Cuba, which is the legalization of the dollar in August 1993. Previously, although dollars circulated in the black market, it was a crime for Cubans to possess dollars. What is your reaction to the government decision to decriminalize the possession of dollars?

Conservative estimates say that there are some $100 million circulating in the black market. The decriminalization of the dollar is an attempt to bring these dollars into the legal economy, which is a good idea.

However, one of the problems is that at this point, most goods sold in dollars — including meat and vegetables — are imported. This means that most of the money will go just to cover the cost of those imports and only a small percentage will be pumped back into the economy.

Another problem is the added social tension and econonic inequalities that this measure will bring about. People with access to dollars — such as those who work in the tourist industry or people with relatives abroad — will enjoy a much higher standard of living than people without dollars, which is the majority of the population. It is no longer the case that those who contribute most to society, such as doctors and engineers and professors, will be the best rewarded.

The way out of the current crisis is not simply to stop inflation. That sounds like Milton Friedman and his Chicago boys to me. The issue here is how to recover production. That requires not only material incentives to producers, but also a new vision of the role of the state and the private sector in the economy.

Isn't this happening with the opening up of some 100 jobs — from plumber to beautician to computer programmer — in which Cubans can work for themselves? While they must be licensed by the state and are not allowed to hire others, this does signal an opening toward more private enterprise.

Yes, both the decriminalization of the dollar and the openings for becoming self-employed point to a reestablishment of the private sector. You can now get capital from relatives abroad, buy tools and raw materials and start your own small business. This is undoubtedly a qualitatively new change, representing a break from the past in which the state has been basically the sole employer. But it is not clear yet what kinds of limits and restrictions will be imposed on these initiatives. I just hope it will not end up being too little, too late.

On the other hand, if Cuba goes down the free enterprise road too far, too fast, there is the danger of losing the socialist nature of the revolution.

This leads us to an even larger question, which is, what is socialism? What is the essence of socialism that we want to save? Traditionally, socialism has been characterized by a centralized, planned economy versus a capitalist unplanned economy. But socialism is not simply a question of a planned economy, because there is a lot of planning in the West as well. In fact, there was more planning in the West than in the Soviet Union. The Japanese do more and better planning than the Russians or the Poles or the Czechs ever did. In the United States, every major corporation has a strategic plan. Some 60-80 percent of the economies in the West are planned by the state or by the large corporations.

We do, however, have a different concept of the market. We don't believe blindly in the laws of supply and demand. We don't believe the market forces should determine if you have a right to

have a roof over your head, if you have a right to see a doctor, if
you have a right to a university education. There are things we
believe should never be submitted to market forces. The basic
human needs of all citizens should not be left to blind market
forces. We believe that human beings and their dignity are above
the market; that the right to life is more important than the "free
market", which, by the way, is not that free anymore anywhere in
the world.

So we can be flexible in other areas, but we must maintain
redistribution of wealth according to socialist principles.

Socialism and its alternatives

Why do you think socialism in the Eastern bloc failed?

Socialism promised a more humane way to organize society; it
promised a society that was not only free from misery but also
free from alienation. Somehow this promise was broken, and the
socialist countries became just another path to industrialization.
They didn't construct an alternative culture and ethical value
system to the consumer societies of the West. I think they were
ethically superior to many capitalist societies in terms of
distribution, but they had nevertheless assimilated from the
bourgeois cultures a series of values based fundamentally on the
philosophy of having, on the philosophy of consumption, and not
on the philosophy of being, not in the ethic of being. Their
cultures were virtually indistinguishable from those in developed
capitalist societies. So when people in both the East and West
were motivated by consumerism, the best consumer society won
out.

Socialism must be much more than a fairer distribution of
resources. Che Guevara used to say that communism was not
only about a better redistribution of goods, but about freeing
people from alienation. If you're going to have a technocratic or
bureaucratic sector replacing the bourgeoisie, then you haven't
dealt with the issue of alienation. You are just having a new
system of domination with fairer distribution. That's not the way

Che or Fidel looked at socialism.

The essence of Che's thinking and his criticism of the socialist bloc are well known. Che wrote back in the 1960s about a major crisis coming in the Eastern bloc, and he predicted that socialism in those countries would collapse if they did not change paths.

Che believed it was not just a question of rapid industrialization or of bringing more technology and consumer goods to the people. What Che called for was a new culture that was based on new types of ethics and values — values different from a capitalist society based on exploitation, racism and greed. You cannot build a society based on ethics and love if the culture is rooted in selfishness and egotism, if it is a "dog-eat-dog" culture.

The kind of socialism we are aiming for has not been known yet in the world. That's the historical significance of our struggle at this very moment in the history of humanity.

Some people say that Cuba's present policy of opening its doors to foreign capital is bringing back all the negative capitalist values of greed and selfishness. Cuba boasts that it has some 100 joint ventures with foreigners, and plans for more in the future. Doesn't this bring back a capitalist ethos?

I would disagree. We are trying to restructure our economy while keeping the essence of the revolution intact. The joint ventures in Cuba are totally different from the type of joint ventures you find in countries like Guatemala or Mexico or Taiwan. They are not joint ventures with foreigners and Cuban individuals, but with the Cuban state. And whatever profit the Cuban state makes, it goes back into the social redistribution of wealth in the form of health care, education, etc.

The foreigners can have 50 percent ownership or more. Our laws have been rewritten so that foreigners can even manage companies. But the labor laws are good — Cuban workers in the joint venture companies have the same benefits as other Cuban workers. Foreigners do have, however, more flexibility when it comes to firing workers. Remember that firing someone in Cuba is, in reality, transferring the worker to another job, not leaving the worker unemployed.

In the past, with the paternalistic socialist approach, workers who were not fulfilling their responsibilities could go on forever without any kind of punishment. The Cuban revolution has been obsessed with the issue of incentives, with the carrots — material or moral — but we have not talked enough about the sticks. Even Che Guevara, who promoted the idea of moral incentives over material incentives, had a carefully planned system of penalties that included the firing and transfer of workers who did not deliver, or docking of pay if they didn't complete the norm.

Are there more traditional communist thinkers in Cuba who are against this policy of working with capitalists?

The issue of opening the economy to foreign capitalist enterprises and individual investors has not been very controversial in Cuba because most people understand that the other markets and sources of investment we used to have are wiped out, leaving us no choice but to become integrated into the Western market. So the debate has not been so much around whether or not to open the economy to this kind of investment. The debate has been around issues such as what kind of regulations should be placed on foreign investors and in what sectors should these investors be allowed to invest.

Hasn't one of the biggest problems in the Cuban economy been that the state controls almost everything? There is a small private sector in farming, with individual farmers and private farm cooperatives. There are now these joint ventures with foreign capital. There is more leeway for individuals to get licenses to work for themselves, and of course there is an entire underground "free market" economy where people make their living off the black market. But the vast majority of economic activities continue to be run by the state, and not very efficiently.

I agree that this is a problem. In my humble opinion, the state should not run every little shop, but should dictate the general direction of the economy. I think there could be small, individually or collectively owned businesses, and we could find alternative models in industry to have workers directly taking responsibility for their workplace. Capitalism itself has a number of different arrangements for that purpose, such as franchising or leasing, that we should carefully examine.

In state-run factories, I think we also have to find a way for the workers to have more say in the daily operation of the factory. Even capitalism is looking more and more towards open management to try to make the workers in a certain enterprise feel like they are owners, even if they are not. So if capitalism is looking for ways to make workers feel part of the company and to make them work more efficiently, then socialism — a system in which the workers own, through the state, the means of production — should have a better way of making workers feel directly responsible for whatever they are doing in their own factory.

If the state is regulating the overall performance of the transactions, if enterprises operate with a sense of the common good and social responsibility, and if you are not allowing differences of income to go beyond a certain limit, I don't believe there should be grounds for concern. The disagreement is with those who blindly believe in the magic bullet of the so-called free market to solve all of our problems. There is an ongoing discussion about this within Cuba right now, and a decision one way or another will have to be taken in the near future. I just hope that market fundamentalism does not capture our imagination.

How do you respond to the critique of socialism from the point of efficiency of production? Some would say that most people in the world, for most of the past 500 years, have been motivated to produce by the threat of losing their job, losing their income, having their family suffer. If you have a constitutional framework where people are guaranteed jobs and guaranteed these various social services, as a human right, then workers will not work as hard as they would if they were under the threat of being fired.

the desire for more?

You're exactly right, that's the way capitalism motivates the working class. The motivation is the "stick" — the threat of being fired, the threat of being homeless, the threat of being hungry or having your children go hungry.

I don't think socialism should back down from guaranteeing people their basic human needs as a way to improve efficiency. But undoubtedly, socialism must develop some other forms of motivation, it must encourage the sense of identification people have with the factory or the farm so they feel that their workplace really belongs to them.

One of the most crucial problems — both economic and political — that socialism all over the world has faced is that the decision-making structures of state-socialism alienate the worker from the workplace. It may be a different kind of alienation than under capitalism, but it is alienation nonetheless. Workers felt that the factory didn't really belong to them, but to the state, a state that supposedly belonged to them also, but in a vague, remote way.

So we have to find new ways through which workers can really have a say in terms of the management and running of their workplaces. They have to feel, in their everyday lives, the consequences of good or bad decisions and performance. They must have real control, and know that their material situation is directly related to the output of the factory or the farm. Otherwise, workers feel they're producing for someone else, for some external entity. So socialism should not start using hunger as a stick to threaten workers with, but must develop a different sense of ownership and responsibility than state socialism has been able to generate.

Why hasn't this happened already in Cuba?

One of the problems is still the legacy of the Soviet model and even worse, the habit of dogmatic thinking. Even when we copied their model, we tried to institute some aspects of popular participation for workers. The model operated on the basis of vertical command; it was hard for institutions such as unions to really develop efficient, participatory democracy in the workplace.

With all our weaknesses, there is still more worker participation in Cuba than in many capitalist societies. In the United States there is no participation of the workers in planning. The CEOs of the Fortune 500 companies have more decision-making power than the 535 representatives in Congress. They can decide tomorrow to shut down a factory in Detroit, affecting thousands of families, and nothing can be done in Congress to prevent it. In our case we have the ability to discuss such scenarios at both the local and national levels before making a decision.

In any case, the kind of democratic planning that we would like to see in the factories and workplaces is not in place and requires much more work to reach a process of collective decision-making by rank and file workers.

Some Cuba watchers say that Cuba is moving towards the Chinese model, with a more open economic system but a tightly controlled political system. Would you agree with this analysis?

We already copied the Soviet model and it would be a great mistake for us to try to copy another model. Of course there are many things we can learn from the Chinese, just as there are many things we can learn from the United States. But the very notion of copying a foreign model makes it impossible to find the right answers to the Cuban reality. Chinese and Cuban people are very different. The history of authoritarian rule in China comes from the Mandarins and ancient history and you need strong vertical authority to carry out some of those experiments.

In any case, I have my own personal doubts about the Chinese experiments, because I am not sure that you can create a market economy and keep the current political system in power at the same time. I see a contradiction there. But I would simply say that we have sent missions to China to study their system. Some of the things they are doing might be of some use in Cuba, but the notion of replicating another model is unwelcome.

Our challenge is to design a more flexible, efficient economic system that does not bring back inequalities and social injustice. There are economic policies — such as those the Chinese are experimenting with — that might lead to short-term prosperity, but could be ruinous in the long run. And this fear is what has been stopping a number of changes from taking place sooner in Cuba.

Dissent and revolution

You may reject the Chinese model, but it seems that Cuba is willing to be much more flexible in the economic sphere than in the political one. Take the issue of dissent. People are allowed to criticize different policies or say negative things about the revolution, but as soon as they start to hold meetings or try to organize, they usually wind up in jail. Some of the critics are people who would like to see the revolution overthrown, others call themselves revolutionaries but say they have a different conception of what the revolution should be. Why isn't the revolution more open to other voices?

Let me first say that there is dissent in all societies — capitalist and socialist — and there are two types of dissent. There is dissent within the system, and this can be dissent about a particular policy or even dissent against a government in power at a given moment, and then there is dissent against the system itself. In the United States, the Democrats and the Republicans disagree on particular policies as a matter of course, but these disagreements fall well within the system. And then you have anti-systemic dissenters who want to change the United States from a capitalist system to a socialist one. In Cuba you also have people who are unhappy with a particular policy and then people who want to see Cuba change from a socialist to a capitalist system.

The Western, capitalist societies, as they have become older and stronger, have an easier time accommodating both kinds of dissent than have socialist societies or Third World capitalist societies. With respect to dissent within the system, they have discovered that it gives society a plurality of options that help self-correct policies that might not be in the interest of the system as a whole.

In these developed capitalist societies, which I call market democracies, even anti-systemic dissenters do not necessarily have to be restrained by a law or by physical coercion — unless they really start to endanger the system. But there is usually an easier way to deal with dissenters, which is to marginalize them economically, to place them in a disadvantaged position. You are limited by your limited access to money. People who have large financial resources are the ones who prevail for the simple fact that they have the ability to influence and shape public opinion through the major media. And those who have a different opinion are marginalized by the simple fact that they don't have the resources to have a major impact or the cultural environment to promote their views. Instead, they have to contend with brainwashed citizens who accept the system and perceive radical dissenters as irrational. These capitalist societies reduce people to what Marcuse called the one dimensional man. While outwardly appearing to be tolerant, they are really totalitarian cultural environments.

The result is that the system allows you to preach to the converted — period. You can distribute leaflets, print your little newsletter, organize small events, but you can rarely reach the major media and if you do, it will be in such a marginal way that it only serves to legitimate the mainstream news by giving the appearance of tolerance for alternative views while denying them the possibility of having a real impact.

Then there are what I call low-intensity democracies, the kind of democracies you find in Central and South America, for example. In these low-intensity democracies, dissenters against the system live in great peril. They are constantly harassed, and may very well be whisked away in the middle of the night, never to be seen again. Dissent within the system is also very limited. Why? Since the system is unable to fulfill its population's basic needs and therefore unable to give the majority of the people a stake in the system, the system is weak and vulnerable and afraid of dissent.

And then there's the example of the Japanese internment camps

in the United States during World War II, showing that even countries that have a high level of development can get quite restrictive when they feel threatened.

Yes, the Japanese were thrown into concentration camps in U.S. territory not even for dissenting but just for the crime of being Japanese and therefore "suspicious" of cooperating with the enemy. While this is not something to condone, it's easy to understand how it happens. Imagine that it's 1941, you're living in San Francisco, and your son was just killed by the Japanese in the bombing of Pearl Harbor. Then you discover that your neighbor is passing out propaganda in favor of the Japanese and you also hear the voice of Tokyo Rose speaking out against the United States. You're going to get very angry.

Or look at how the United States treated dissenters immediately after its independence. Out of the four million inhabitants in 1776, around 100,000 were expatriated and sent back to England. Their return was banned and all their properties were confiscated without any compensation. At a time when one-third of the population of the 13 colonies remained loyal to His Majesty George III, it was declared a crime against the nation to print false, scandalous or malicious material against the government or to promote sedition or to cooperate with any foreign power against the United States.

Well, some of the intolerance that you see in Cuba toward the dissenters against the system has to do with the perception that these dissenters are allied with a powerful foreign country that has been hostile to us for over 100 years. If Americans were more sensitive to their own history, they might be more understanding of ours.

In the last 35 years, we suffered through an invasion, a Missile Crisis, assassination plots, spying and sabotage by the United States. We are a tiny island 90 miles away from *the* superpower, not *a* superpower — the only superpower in the world. And if that weren't enough, we have a U.S. military base right on our island — the Guantánamo Naval Base.

So try to put yourself in the shoes of a Cuban today. We are being strangled economically, we are subjected to a blockade that is stopping us from getting medicines and milk for our children. Imagine hearing your neighbor on the U.S.-financed Radio Martí saying that he is in favor of the blockade. You get very angry.

But it is one thing to get angry, and another thing to abuse people merely because they disagree with your political views. The Rapid Response Brigades, neighborhood groups created to stop dissenters from organizing, have been known to get very abusive with neighbors whom they believe are counter-revolutionaries.

When people get angry, they often lose control. Remember how civilized Europeans dragged naked women by their hair in the streets of Paris for having a love affair with a Nazi soldier. No one in my country has ever committed such brutal excesses.

I myself am a member of the Rapid Response Brigade in my building. It's true there have been cases where such encounters have gotten out of hand. I joined the brigade precisely because I think it is important to make sure that there will be no excesses or abuses. I feel it's essential to keep the respect for human dignity that we professed toward our enemies in the days when we fought Batista's forces in the Sierra Maestra or mercenary invaders during the Bay of Pigs.

But not everyone everywhere reacts the same way. It is not in the interest of the Cuban government to mistreat dissidents, since that is what the international media would immediately focus on and exaggerate. But it is not always possible for the government to control such situations. In fact, when there are fights between revolutionaries and counterrevolutionaries, you see the police stepping in to stop the dissidents from being abused.

Look, the United States has applied every trick in the book against Cuba. Techniques that were later applied in El Salvador or against the Nicaraguan government were applied previously in Cuba — contras in the mountains, bombings, everything. We are dealing with an undeclared war that the United States is waging against us.

So obviously you don't get the kind of tolerant environment you might find in Switzerland. You get a kind of anger, a kind of intolerance in dealing with dissent. In fact, I would say that the conservatives in the United States, with their hard line against Cuba, reinforce extreme reactions in Havana. A relaxation of the way that dissenters against the system are perceived would require a relaxation in the international environment so that we could accommodate dissenting views against the system in a different way.

You make a distinction between dissent within the system and anti-systemic dissenters. How has Cuba historically treated dissent within the system, and has the recent crisis and hostile international environment narrowed the space for such dissent?

One of the historic problems with socialism around the world is that it never came to terms with accommodating dissent within the system. I know this firsthand because I have been, if you wish, a "dissident" within the revolution on many issues and for quite a long time.

Can you give us some specific examples?

In the late 1960s I was teaching in the department of philosophy at the university. The department was a center for all kinds of creative thinking about socialism, and we published a magazine called *Pensamiento Critico*, or Critical Thought. We were trying to create a Cuban Marxist school of thinking, using a non-dogmatic approach to Marxism. As Che Guevara suggested, we approached Marxism "with the natural attitude that somebody in physics might embrace Newton, without declaring Newton the last word in physics."

Throughout the 1960s, we tried to update the Cuban population on the major trends of thinking of our time. *Pensamiento Critico* was the kind of magazine that would have been frowned upon in the Soviet Union because it included all different schools of thought, including bourgeois thought (which is, of course, one of the major schools of thought in modern times), liberal thinking, radical socialist thinking. You could read the writings of African Amilcar Cabral next to the works of the

German Herbert Marcuse, and of course we would include Cuban thinkers as well. We also included critiques of the Soviet model. All this was something totally "abnormal" for a proper, prudent Soviet socialist publication.

This experiment lasted until the end of the decade, when the Russification of the Cuban model began and derailed a number of original efforts like the one at our university. All of a sudden the direction of the department changed, a new curriculum was imposed, and *Pensamiento Critico* was shut down.

I was not in favor of copying the Soviet model and made my views known. I refused to teach Soviet Marxism; I could not lie to my students saying something to them that I didn't believe in. So I had to quit my teaching job.

Did anything else happen to you?

No, I did not end up in prison or anything like that, and I was able to get a job elsewhere. But during that time there was little room for public debate on issues like this.

Amazingly enough, there is more room for debate today. There are openings today that did not exist 10 years ago. The existence of the non-governmental organization I am now heading is a testament to that. The very existence of my institution, a non-government institution for the study of politics and ethics, would have been unthinkable 10 years ago. This is because according to the Soviet model, every non-governmental organization, with the exception of the mass organizations promoted by the system itself, was perceived as suspicious.

I find it very encouraging that during the most difficult moment in the revolution's history, we are moving toward a more pluralistic view of the construction of socialism. At one time the line of the party was *the* line — period — and if you spoke against that line, no matter how respectfully, you were perceived as a counterrevolutionary. This is not the case anymore. Within the party there is a growing trend for presenting alternative views and airing differences. So the logic that is prevailing today is not the logic of repression but the logic of democracy.

The admission of religious believers into the party and into high posts of government, which happened at the Fourth Party Congress in 1991, was an important step. Perhaps more important than what it meant to the believers themselves is the psychological impact it had of opening the society to more points of views. These are, of course, views within the system, because they are religious people who in one way or another back up the system. Like anyone else, they may disagree with particular policies, but they believe in building a socialist society. So we are moving little by little into a policy of more flexibility.

We are starting to understand that democracy is not a luxury, it is a necessity. If we want to save the system, we need to guarantee a plurality of views.

If there was, indeed, a more open environment prevailing, you would expect to see this reflected in the Cuban press. Yet the press continues to be abysmal. Year after year, there are conferences in which everyone speaks out about the need to have a more investigative press, a more interesting press, a more dynamic press. But despite all these criticisms and calls for change at all levels of the Cuban society, nothing changes. Why?

One of the problems of copying the Eastern bloc model is the role that was given to the press. It is more apologetic than investigative journalism. I feel you can have investigative journalism from a revolutionary point of view without giving up your ideals and values. The problem is that this is not the way the media has been perceived in Cuba and it's not the role the media has been playing.

On the other hand, with all the TV and radio that comes from the United States, you can't say that Cuba is closed to the Western media. You can hear some 15 Miami radio stations. And in terms of TV, if you walk around Havana you will see all over town these little square antennas on people's roofs. Everyone knows that these are for receiving UHF stations from Miami, because there are no UHF stations in Cuba. The very fact that those antennas are tolerated, that nobody knocks on your door to question you about your antenna, shows that we are not a closed society.

So it's not that the Cuban people are uninformed, it's that they are ill-informed. They either get an apologetic point of view from the national media, or a totally distorted view from Miami. Either way, the press is not objective in its coverage of Cuban affairs.

We certainly need to create a more objective press in Cuba, a press that could play a role in the economic and political restructuring of the country by providing insights, by providing ideas, by being a communication vessel between ordinary Cuban citizens and the central government. That is a necessity. But it's blocked by many prejudices from the past, and the international environment certainly doesn't help. It is difficult to create another kind of journalism without a change in the international environment.

Leadership and transition

It seems that a factor that makes it difficult to foster alternative views in Cuba is the incredibly strong role played by Fidel Castro. People must not be very anxious to put out views that are opposed to those of Fidel.

People in the West, whatever their political persuasion, seem to overestimate the role of Fidel Castro in decision-making in Cuba. I have already described the different stages of development we have gone through, and each stage has been ascribed to a particular group within the leadership or within the party. We might not have different political parties, but we do have different visions within the same party about how to construct socialism. On some occasions, Fidel Castro has been identified with the prevailing vision. On other occasions, as in the 1970s and early 1980s, he did not agree with the predominant vision, even though he remained head of the Council of State. Fidel Castro is a national leader, he must unify the different trends to provide national leadership, which might often mean giving up his particular vision to play that unifying role.

This misperception about Fidel is similar to the tendency among historians in the West to overstate the role of individuals as makers of history. I believe that individuals and their ideas have an incredible impact on history, and certainly no one can write the history of the Cuban revolution without taking into account the personality of Fidel Castro. But Fidel Castro would not have been able to lead the revolution unless the international and national situation was propitious. He decided, for example, that it was proper to land in Cuba with 82 men to defeat an army of 72,000 that was backed up by the United States. It may sound nutty, but he was right because he correctly assessed the spirit of the Cuban population at that time and he correctly assessed the international correlation of forces and the possibilities that existed to make the revolution viable. So there is a balance between individuals and history, between the objective process of history and the individual making history.

Whatever the proper emphasis on the individual in history, it is undeniable that Fidel Castro is an historical figure who comes once a century — if that. It would certainly take a strong figure to replace Fidel, especially during what will most likely continue to be extremely difficult times. Who do you think might replace Fidel? We used to hear a lot of talk about his brother, Raúl, but you don't hear that anymore. Now we hear talk of people like Roberto Robaina, who used to be the Communist Youth leader and is now foreign minister. Or Ricardo Alarcón, who used to be foreign minister and is now head of the National Assembly. Or Carlos Lage, the pediatrician who runs the economy. Who might be a likely successor?

I don't think there are any individuals who could replace Fidel Castro. He could only be replaced by collective leadership, by institutions. If anyone thinks he or she can become another Fidel Castro, we're in big trouble, because no one would have the same legitimacy. The kind of leadership that Fidel has provided comes from his historic role, which is a unique one.

I do feel, though, that Fidel is very serious when he

commented to Diane Sawyer on U.S. television in early 1993 that he would like to step aside from his current position. And he's not saying this in reaction to U.S. pressure. We don't yield on matters of sovereignty to external pressures. I believe that Fidel would really like to witness, in his lifetime, another generation coming to lead the country in the right direction.

And this means that the revolution must nurture a group of new leaders, and that is precisely what is happening with the people whose names you mentioned, and others. These are all people of a younger generation.

Could you comment on the significance of Ricardo Alarcón being transferred from the post of foreign minister to head of the National Assembly? Some Cuba watchers have interpreted it as a demotion.

On the contrary. I see it as a serious attempt to give more weight to the National Assembly. Alarcón is a capable, well-respected leader in Cuba and he will give the new assembly a new stature in Cuban politics. I will expect him to still play a major role in foreign policy, but now from his position as president of the assembly.

And what about the appointment of Roberto Robaina to foreign minister? I was shocked to hear that a 38-year-old youth leader, with virtually no experience in foreign affairs, would be given this role at such a critical time.

The appointment of Robaina took many people by surprise because we have perceived Robaina as a youth leader. And when you are a youth leader, the kind of speeches you deliver and the informal way you act — going around in jeans and sneakers — is in contrast to the formal image you have in foreign affairs. His appointment sends a clear message — both internally and externally — that a new transition of leadership has started.

It's so hard to imagine the Cuban revolution without Fidel at the helm. How would you feel about Fidel leaving power?

First let me say that, luckily for us, Fidel is in good health. He doesn't go around fainting at Japanese banquets like George Bush did. But, of course, we are all aware that one day he will not be with us anymore.

Fidel Castro will be remembered by everyone, friends and foes alike. He is one of those unusual personalities who change the course of history. Many will be forever grateful for the ways in which he has changed history, others will hate him for the same deeds. But even many of his enemies have learned, as decent adversaries always do, to admire and respect both his genius and his integrity.

To me his absence would be a personal source of sadness as well as a permanent source of inspiration. That's how I also feel about Che Guevara. They are both irreplaceable.

Fidel is to me like a very close and respected relative. Since my childhood, in the days of the war in the Sierra Maestra, I clung to the radio at night to hear his voice reassuring us that we would defeat Batista. For more than three decades I have turned to him again and again for direction — during those days of the Bay of Pigs invasion, the Missile Crisis, and the many other dramatic and critical situations in which our very lives were at stake. I don't see him as a God but as an individual with exceptional talents and an extraordinary sense of ethics.

While I have not agreed with him on every issue, I've agreed with him on every major topic. And most important, I've learned that history has proven him right almost without exception.

Fidel and Che recaptured humanism for Marxists and socialists. Maybe that's their major contribution to humanity as we are entering the Third Millennia.

I respect what you say about Fidel, yet it is hard for me as an outsider to not get the feeling of a personality cult. There are so many things that have gone wrong in the Cuban revolution — things like the overdependence on the Soviet bloc that is causing such pain and suffering today and may yet be the undoing of the revolution. Yet you blame all the bad on Fidel not getting his way and give Fidel credit for all the good. It's not very rational, and you are a very rational man. But I suppose it is difficult to criticize a leader who is still in power and a leader who today — more than ever — represents the glue that is keeping the revolution together.

But if Fidel Castro still retains so much legitimacy in the eyes of many Cubans, why won't he submit himself to an election? This would be a way to prove to the outside world that the people continue to support the revolution and it would give Fidel so much more international legitimacy.

I find it very strange that the Western media either ignored or misinterpreted the elections for the National Assembly that we had in December 1992. If they had really looked closely at the process, they would have realized that this was also, aside from an election, a referendum on Fidel Castro and on the revolution.

I know that some Cubans don't like this thesis because they feel that it downplays the election as such, but in my own personal judgment, it was both an election and a referendum.

First of all, in 1992 the electoral laws were changed to call for the direct election of representatives to the National Assembly, which is the equivalent of your Congress. Previously, the people chose the local representatives out of a slate of several candidates. The winners then elected the provincial representatives, who then elected the national representatives. So these direct national elections were the first of their kind.

While there were several candidates to choose from at the local level, in these national elections there was only one set of candidates. You could delete the name of anyone on the list, you could choose all of them, or you could make your vote a protest vote by spoiling the ballot or leaving it blank.

Now to understand the significance of this campaign, you must understand that in the middle of our crisis, Cubans were bombarded by radio stations in Miami with messages calling on them to nullify their ballots. This was a major campaign in Miami, with about 15 stations broadcasting 24 hours a day. They spent literally thousands of hours of broadcasting time urging Cubans not to vote or to leave their ballot blank. Radio Martí alone broadcast 452 messages about the elections.

In response to this campaign, the government then asked the

people to support the revolution by giving a united vote as a patriotic response and as a way of keeping the revolutionary vote united. Every vote was important and people were aware of that. You could still pick one individual and not another, but the population was asked to give a yes to the whole list of candidates. Fidel himself went all over the country explaining the measure and the importance of voting for the unified slate, and he himself was a candidate in the city of Santiago. So Fidel really put himself on the line during this vote, and remember that we are talking about an election that was taking place during our most severe economic crisis.

What I find curious is that for years the U.S. government and the counterrevolutionary forces have been pressing for a referendum on Fidel Castro. And that is essentially what happened, but no one wanted to recognize this. This was not a referendum on particular policies — because many people would like to see a number of policies changed — but it did transform itself into a referendum on sovereignty, on the revolution, on Fidel Castro, on socialism as a path for national liberation. People were voting both for a slate of candidates and for the continuity of the revolutionary process as the right path to face and surmount the current situation.

And what was the outcome?

The interesting thing is that in the solitude of the booth — booths that were checked out by the international media, the diplomatic corps and neighborhood committees — people overwhelmingly voted in favor of the revolution and against the Miami option.

Almost 99.6 percent of eligible voters actually voted, and voting is not mandatory. The votes were counted in public, before the neighbors and international observers. In the city of Havana — where most of the problems are more acute — about 15 percent nullified their vote. Nationally, only 7.2 percent of the population nullified their ballot.

But let's use our imagination in order to understand the significance of the outcome. Let's say that 1 percent of the people didn't vote. Let's also be conservative and take the percentage of spoiled votes in Havana — 15 percent — and say that was the national average. Let's also assume that all Cubans overseas voted — another million people — and that all these Cubans overseas voted against the revolution (which would not be the case). You would still have the revolution backed up by over 75 percent of the population.

I would like to see a government in the United States elected with the participation of 99 percent of the people, and getting a 75 percent backing, especially in a critical economic period.

But at least in the United States people are allowed to openly organize for an alternative. In Cuba's case the only opposition that had a public voice was that coming from Miami.

I think that given the present economic crisis and the constant hostility Cuba faces from the United States, these elections were very significant. In any case, to me elections are not synonymous with democracy but only one aspect of democracy. The West has tried for decades to reduce democracy to the exercise of voting every four years. To me, democracy is the daily input of the population on matters that affect their lives and not simply the casting of a ballot for a menu of candidates backed by powerful forces.

But it is difficult to find an example around the world of one-party systems that allow for open discussion and debate on these very issues that affect people's lives. While there are many imperfections in the democratic models of the West, they do seem to offer more room for alternative voice than socialist societies have. Do you simply dismiss multi-party systems as bourgeois democracies?

On many occasions multi-party systems are identified with pluralism. But that is not necessarily the case; sometimes multi-party systems are precisely the way to *deny* pluralism. In Cuba during the 1900s, we had plenty of political parties but no democracy. For us, the multi-party system consistently denied the possibility of an alternative road for the country.

I am not going to enter into a critique of the U.S. bi-party system. In fact, the founding fathers of your own country did a much better job critiquing such a system than I could. However, I do remember Gore Vidal saying that today the U.S. political system is really a one-party system with two right wings.

I think that one thing socialist states *can* learn from capitalist states is their great flexibility when it comes to "models". The history of the West has been very generous in providing different political systems. You have single chamber and double chamber parliaments, you have parliamentary monarchies. You have multi-party systems like in India, two-party systems like in the United States, or one-party systems, as is virtually the case in Taiwan.

You have kings and queens that no one elected. In Great Britain, the queen has the right to designate a number of people in the House of Lords. In Belgium, you have a king that no one had any say about, in fact it was decided by external forces after the world war, and this king has the right to nominate the head of the government. So the head of the government in Belgium is not elected by anybody, he is designated by a king, who is also not elected by anybody.

Are you comparing Fidel Castro to a king?

I'm not saying that Fidel Castro is a king, among other things because he regularly submits to the ballot box. That's not the way kings behave. I'm just pointing out that in the West nobody is saying that Belgium is not democratic because they have a king or Spain is not democratic because they have a king, or Great Britain is not democratic because they have a queen.

In the West you have all sorts of arrangements, and all of them are considered democracies. There is a double standard: one for Taiwan, one for Guatemala, one for Kuwait, in fact — one for the entire capitalist world — and a different one for Cuba.

What was stupid before, in the history of socialism, is that socialism was narrowly and dogmatically defined as only the Soviet model. All other socialist countries had to copy that model. Socialism does not necessarily have to be organized in any particular way; it does not necessarily have to be a one-party state or a multi-party system. It could even create a new political system for itself, a system that has never been tried before. The very same way that capitalism has consistently adapted its political and economic systems to different national realities, so must socialism.

Would you be in favor of a multi-party system in Cuba?

I do not dogmatically believe in the one-party system or in any other arrangement. But remember, we did not copy our one-party system from the Soviets. It was really a legacy of José Martí's attempt to create one party out of several parties that existed at the end of the last century. All of them were independent clubs in conflict with one another — parties were called clubs at that time — and Martí wanted to bring all of those little parties into one huge party in which they could co-exist with their own points of view and visions but be united in their efforts to achieve independence.

In terms of the future of the Cuban political system, our system is not and could never be a finished product; it is something that is in process. It has emerged at a particular time in history and is evolving according to the history of our country, the psychology of our people, and the environment that surrounds us.

To make this more understandable for an American reader, take the history of the United States. In your country, democracy the way you know it now was not the way it was born in 1776. Your democratic system was born with 40 million slaves who did not participate in voting. As a matter of fact, the Blacks were not able to truly participate until the civil rights movement in the 1960s. Women did not participate in voting until the 1920s.

After your revolution, there was no party system. It was in 1791 that the first party was founded, which was the Federalist Party. And the first election with two parties — although not yet parties in the modern sense — took place in 1796 when George Washington left office. The real first elections with modern alternative parties took place in 1820.

Over all those years, the founding fathers of your country —

George Washington, Benjamin Franklin, Thomas Jefferson — they were all against the party system. Even James Monroe spoke as late as 1816 against a party system, stating that "the existence of parties is not necessary to free governments." Some people in the industrial north were promoting a party system, and the founding fathers claimed that this was divisive, that it was going to divide the nation and make it vulnerable to Great Britain and to the great powers in Europe. The founding fathers argued that it was crucial to keep the revolution together, and it was a bad idea to create parties that would compete for power and divide the American society. They refered pejoratively to parties as factions.

Obviously, that changed later on. The system evolved when the new leaders felt less vulnerable to outside powers and also felt that a party system would better serve the management of the conflicting interests in the newly emerged nation. It slowly evolved from a non-party system to a one-party system to a two-party system.

Cuba, as an historical reality, is also evolving into the future. I am not saying that the best possible political system is the one we have now. It is the system we have in this particular time in history, which doesn't mean that it cannot change tomorrow if internal and external conditions change. But the kind of society in which we are living — threatened by a great superpower — is not the most likely one to have a relaxed, tolerant, flexible environment to carry on democracy the way it might be carried out in Switzerland.

Are you saying that if the international tension eased, you would like to see Cuba evolve into a multi-party system?

Not necessarily. I'm not saying that the absence of a multi-party system in Cuba is a deficiency due to the limitations of our present circumstances. In fact, rather than advocating an evolution toward a multi-party system, which is a system that emerged in the world some 200 years ago as a response to a specific historical reality, I would prefer to see us create a new kind of democracy using different tools. I think it is entirely possible to achieve a pluralist one-party system if in that system there were strong sectoral organizations — women's organizations, farmers groups, neighborhood committees, etc. These sectoral organizations exist in Cuba today, but would have to be stronger at the grassroots level to play the role, when necessary, of challenging government policies.

In summary, I don't have in mind the exact system I would like to see evolve in Cuba, but I am enthusiastic about the idea of building an entirely new, revolutionary model to fit our revolutionary society.

Revolution and discrimination

Included in the issue of allowing for more points of view is not just the issue of political points of view, but religious beliefs and sexual orientation. Could you talk about how the revolution has dealt with both the religious and the gay communities?

Unfortunately, all revolutions commit mistakes; they commit excesses and abuses. Take the French or American revolutions: if you read Mark Twain on the American revolutionary experience, we will see the kinds of excesses that occurred.

In our case, we, too, committed mistakes and excesses, particularly in the early years when we had to defend ourselves from counterrevolutionary forces. One group that we mistakenly discriminated against was religious believers. We inherited from the Soviets this mistaken notion that there was a contradiction between religion and revolution. Religious believers were not allowed to enter certain careers or to hold certain positions in the government. Many of these people left for the United States because their lives were made very difficult in Cuba. The majority stayed, hoping that better times would come.

In the history of Cuba, religious believers were often involved in the struggle for social justice. José Martí himself was a believer, and we had Catholic priests fighting against Spain and later against Batista. So it was crazy for us to have this notion that a religious position was counterrevolutionary.

Today, discrimination against religious believers is a thing of the past. People of religious faith can enter the Communist Party. We now even have religious delegates in the National Assembly, our highest legislative body.

Let's go on to the issue of the gay community. The worst period was one year in the 1960s when gay people were thrown into reeducation camps. It's been a long time since that kind of repression happened, but gays still don't seem to be accepted in Cuban society.

Cuba is a Latino, machista culture. We didn't get this from the revolution — we inherited this culture from Spain. But we had a certain Calvinist, puritanical notion of morality during the 1960s that made the revolution repressive against gays. By the 1970s, repression as such stopped, but discrimination prevailed. We are just now dealing with this issue.

It was at the Fourth Party Congress in 1991 that it was decided that religious believers could be members of the Communist Party. Yet there is still a restriction on gays joining the party. If Cuba is indeed opening space for the gay community, why wasn't this issue brought up?

Maybe the party congress was not ready to face two sensitive issues at once. I think Sigmund Freud was right when he said that sexuality is more sensitive than politics. There is still the widespread notion in Cuba that homosexuality is a deviation, a perversion. The nature of homosexual love is not understood.

I don't have to embrace someone's sexual preference to understand their right to have options. But one of the problems in openly discussing homosexual rights is that even if you yourself are not a homosexual, if you defend homosexual rights people will label you a homosexual. The fear of facing this accusation is paralyzing many people.

Fortunately, though, we are making some headway. You can now find plays about homosexuality in the theater. Vilma Espín, head of the Federation of Cuban Women, has stressed that homosexuality is not a perversion. Fidel Castro, in a widely publicized interview he granted to Tomás Borge [published as *Face to face with Fidel Castro*], said he was totally opposed to any kind of discrimination against homosexuals, and that homosexuality is simply a natural tendency that must be respected.

It is extremely important that high-level leaders are saying that communist morality is not to be confused with homophobia. We have to continue this struggle through the intellectual community, the youth organizations, the women's federation, the media. The revolution has dealt seriously with racial and gender discrimination. It is time to deal seriously with discrimination against the homosexual community.

Some cite continuing discrimination against gays in the way Cuba has dealt with AIDS. There is mandatory testing of at-risk groups and mandatory confinement in a health center until that person has proven that he or she will not infect others.

Our AIDS policy has nothing to do with discrimination against gays but with trying to stop a terrible disease. The majority of people with AIDS in Cuba are heterosexual, not homosexual. As a matter of fact, the West has reinforced discrimination against homosexuals by making AIDS look as if it were basically a homosexual disease.

Our policy might have been seen as restricting individual liberties, at least initially, but it also has many positive features that are not well known. If you are HIV-positive in Cuba, you have your job ensured, you keep receiving your salary whether or not you are able to work. All your treatment is free — and you know that AIDS treatment can be quite expensive. We use interferon, for example, which is extremely expensive.

There is an ethical question about dealing with the restriction of movement. There are certain illnesses in which patients have been historically isolated from the rest of the population — tuberculosis, leprosy. In those cases, people were isolated, but their social rights were not granted — they didn't have a salary, they couldn't sustain their families. Yes, we are restricting people's movement. But once they have a psychological checkup and show that they will not infect others, they can leave the hospital and just return for treatment. But if the psychological team believes that the infected person may infect others, he or she will be kept there. I personally believe that this is justified, for I believe that the right of the rest of the population to remain healthy is more important than total individual freedom.

Another issue that arises when we discuss discrimination is the issue of the Black community in Cuba. The government certainly has no kind of institutional discrimination, and when you visit Cuba, you get a sense of an extremely racially harmonious population. Yet critics such as Carlos Moore, an Afro-Cuban who migrated to the United States, charge that Cuba is a racist society. What do you think?

About half of Cubans are Black. If you compare the social indices of the Black population in Cuba before and after the revolution, you will find that this sector has gained tremendously since the revolution. There are people in the United States who call Cuba racist, but Cubans are the only people in the world who voluntarily went to Africa to fight the racist troops of Pretoria. More than 300,000 Cubans went to Angola, either as soldiers or doctors or engineers or teachers — men and women, black and white. And their goal was to fight against the racism that the CIA was trying to impose in Angola through the white South African mercenaries fighting on the side of Holden Roberto and Jonas Savimbi.

I am not claiming that there is no racism in Cuba. That would be untrue. There is not institutional racism, but there is still evidence of individual racism the very same way that there are prejudices in Cuba against the gay community; the very same way that there is still sexism. Those are realities that have been ingrained for centuries, and you don't wipe them out in 35 years. To twist that around to say that Cuba is a racist country is ridiculous.

In terms of the record of wiping out racism institutionally, I don't think there is a better record in the world than the record of the Cuban revolution.

Revolutionary ethics

One of the major goals of the Cuban revolution was to create "el nuevo hombre," the new person, a person who had a collective rather than an individualist approach to life. The revolution was to promote a morality that did not thrive on selfishness but on working together for the good of all. It seems that during the early years of the revolution, there was more of this collective spirit and that in the present crisis, there is a breakdown of that spirit, as witnessed by the upsurge in prostitution, black marketing, etc.

People in Cuba are reacting to the present economic crisis in different ways. I would say that most Cubans do face the crisis today in a collective manner and with ethical principles. But a minority — unfortunately a growing minority — face the crisis with a selfish, individualist approach. Let me give you an example. At the beginning of the revolution we did away with prostitution. Prostitution is now returning to the city of Havana. You only see it around Havana because it is linked to the presence of tourists. Women prostitutes are not interested in going out with Cuban men, because they want dollars, not Cuban pesos. Cuban women or men don't need to prostitute themselves to get pesos, because the government's policy has been to make sure whatever is available is equally shared and therefore not expensive in Cuban money.

So those who face the crisis with this individualist approach hang around the tourist hotels and try to get tourists to buy them things in the dollar stores. Others resort to stealing. Still others try to flee the crisis by emigrating to the United States.

In my case, we have about seven people in our extended family. We face the problems that all Cubans have been facing — sometimes we can't get soap, we can't get toothpaste, sometimes we don't have cooking oil. But it's unthinkable for us to face the crisis through stealing or prostitution or leaving the country — we face the crisis with collective principles.

I cannot say that all Cubans face the crisis with high ideals, but most do. While more Cubans today may have succumbed to an individualist approach than in the 1960s, they are still a minority.

You make it sound like it's a question of people upholding the highest principles or succumbing to prostitution. Aren't most people in between? I know a lot of people who go to Revolution Square for a rally and shout "socialism or death" and then go home and buy on the black market.

It is not the same to say "al que Dios se lo dio, San Pedro se lo bendiga" (to whom God gives, Saint Peter blesses) as to say "con los pobres de la Tierra quiero yo mi suerte echar" (I want to cast my fate with the poor of the earth). They are two totally different ethical codes. The first one means that different people have different lots in life. It also means that the way that someone's wealth was· acquired is irrelevant. Whether you got wealthy through legal or illegal means is not important. God gave you the ability to somehow acquire that wealth, and that's all that matters.

If someone goes to the Revolution Square and shouts "I want to cast my fate with the poor of the earth" and then goes back home and applies "al que Dios se lo dio...", we are witnessing a phenomenon of ideological interpenetration of two ethical codes in the same person. And this ideological struggle in the mind for the supremacy of one code or another will determine the fate of the Cuban revolution.

If you believe in the revolutionary ideal, you might say, "I don't want to go to the countryside to work in agriculture but I must make the sacrifice to help my country move forward." If you have the other ethical code, you might decide to become a prostitute to get dollars to buy soap. Everyone confronts the crisis according to their value system.

Do you think the Cuban school system is doing a good job of teaching the proper value system to Cuban youth?

Sometimes we mechanically restrict the problem of ethical education to the school system — and this has to do with the double morality in socialist societies. The schools — from elementary school to the university — can transmit a certain system of values, but what good does it do if the social institutions generate another value system, if the economy in its day-to-day workings is not also run by a determined ethical code. It does no good to teach our children a certain ethic in school, if this code is violated everyday in real life — in the workplace, in the shops.

But doesn't the Cuban system impose this kind of schizophrenia? People are asked to be morally pure and live by the highest revolutionary standards. From the time the children start school, they chime the slogan "Seremos como el Che," we'll be like Che. This means, we'll uphold Che's firm sense of social justice and equality for all. We'll uphold the highest revolutionary standards.

Then there's the "real world." And in that world, especially with the shortages of today, people do something illegal almost every day just to "resolver," to get by. People are not starving in Cuba thanks to the black market. A piece of soap? A bottle of shampoo? A pair of shoes? All on the black market. Taking something extra home from work — be it a bit of food or a light bulb or some paper. Everyone does it, and they justify it as necessary to "resolver," to get by. So is the revolution asking too much of people to uphold strict principles at a time when it is almost impossible to do so?

Yes, most people are probably unconsciously battling these two codes every day. In one moment or another they can fall into a disequilibrium in favor of one or the other — altruism or egoism. And when this occurs as a mass phenomenon, it can mean victory or defeat of the revolution. The survival of the revolution not only depends on our ability to surmount the material crisis. It is a question of doing so without changing our souls. I know this is an uphill battle. That is precisely why it deserves respect.

Critics of the revolution say that things like black marketing and crime are some of the only ways to express opposition to

the regime. They say that if Cuba were not such a police state, there would be more and more expressions of dissent which would eventually grow to the point of overthrowing the government.

Those same people who accuse Cuba of being a police state are the ones who said the very same thing about the Soviet Union and Eastern Europe. So if those countries were police states, how come their governments were overthrown and not the Cuban government? Take Poland. People said Poland was a police state, but despite this, a mass movement emerged that overthrew the government. So why hasn't such a movement been able to coalesce in Cuba?

Moreover, there are examples all over the capitalist world where people have risen up against truly repressive systems, putting their lives in extreme peril. Whatever people say about Cuba, the Cuban government does not "disappear" people, like the U.S.-allied governments of Guatemala or El Salvador. Why do the people in these countries, and dozens of others throughout the world, risk their lives to overthrow their governments, while the same kind of mass opposition has not occurred in Cuba despite Cuba's historical tradition of rebellion and insurrection against tyrannies? Surely the level of repression is not the answer, and those who insist that it is the answer simply refuse to acknowledge the level of support that the revolutionary option of development has in Cuba.

I would agree with you that Cuban socialism hasn't crumbled as it did in the Soviet Union and Eastern Europe because the Cuban government has more legitimacy than those governments did. But I would say that an equally important reason is that Cubans don't see a viable alternative. They look at Eastern Europe and the former Soviet Union and see misery and chaos. They look at "Third World" capitalist countries and see hunger and misery. So why overthrow a government if you have no idea of what to put in its place?

On the other hand, how viable is the Cuban revolution? The alternatives may not be bright, but neither are the short- and

medium-term prospects for the revolution.

If you look at Cuba's history, geopolitical factors have always played a role in our destiny. We fought against Spain at the turn of the century, when Spain was a declining power and the United States was a rising power. And that's what allowed us to get free from Spain, but it threw us under the yoke of the United States. In 1959 there was a different geopolitical reality — there was the Soviet Union and the Eastern bloc. While it was not a determining factor in making the revolution, it was a determining factor in the viability of the revolution later on.

Right now we're entering a new geopolitical reality. Some people say that the pendulum has swung backwards, that Cuba now has no geopolitical ally to help confront the American challenge and therefore has no viable future. That's not so accurate. We now see a new conflict within the capitalist world itself — between Japan, Western Europe and the United States. If the United States is so stupid that it doesn't want to make Cuba an ally and respect its sovereignty, then maybe we will find better trading partners in Western Europe and Japan.

We have also built up human and infrastructural resources that make us more viable. We have a consolidated scientific community — about 62 percent are women and the average age of our scientists is 28. We also have an economic infrastructure that is in bad shape, but is there nonetheless — the communication system is there, the ports are there, the harbors are there. There is an accumulation of resources that we now have to face the new geopolitical reality.

We have a strong peoples army that can inflict significant casualties on a U.S. invading force, so that the possibility of a low-intensity conflict with Cuba is virtually out of the question. It would have to be a medium-level conflict, which is something that the planners in the Pentagon have to bear in mind.

And in the end, the most important resource we have is the Cuban people. The very same way that the most important resource the Japanese have is the Japanese. In the final analysis, their most important resource is their brains, their talent. And that is the case of Cuba as well.

Why hasn't the end of the Cold War between the United States and the former Soviet Union led to a thaw in the relations between the United States and Cuba?

As I mentioned earlier, the United States still operates according to the Monroe Doctrine. With the strange concept that it has the right to control its "backyard", the United States has brought much misery to Latin America. The United States has believed that the only way to relate to Latin America was by controlling the reins of power in the hemisphere — controlling the military, the bureaucracy, the state finances, etc.

The kind of domination the United States has exerted in Latin America is totally different in nature from the kind of leadership it provides, for example, in Western Europe. By the time of World War II, the United States had gained a dominant position in international affairs, and it exerted tremendous influence over Western Europe. But increasingly the United States learned to treat the nations of Western Europe as allies, not as pawns or servants.

Today the United States does not try to directly control the internal politics or the militaries of those countries. It has a more flexible, tolerant approach. This means that U.S. leaders do not try to overthrow socialist leaders like Mitterrand in France.

But in Latin America the very same kind of leader would cause U.S. officials to have nightmares. Look at Michael Manley in his first term in Jamaica, or Salvador Allende in Chile. They were socialists, but they were reformists; they were not trying to overthrow the system but to modify it. U.S. leaders nonetheless immediately began plotting how to get them out of power. So obviously U.S. leaders have some kind of intolerance for Latin American sovereignty that is not there when it comes to other areas of the world.

Subjectively speaking, the United States might believe that it is really reacting to communism. But when you look objectively at the reality, the United States has been intolerant of change in Latin America even before the Bolshevik revolution ever existed.

The United States sent the Marines into Nicaragua in 1907. At that time there was no Bolshevik revolution and the person in charge in Nicaragua was not Daniel Ortega, but rather General Zelaya, a reformist. And when the United States intervened throughout the decades in Latin American affairs, they were bringing down leaders who usually had no relationship to either the communist or socialist movements — people like Juan Bosch in the Dominican Republic, Janos Goulart in Brazil, or Jacobo Arbenz in Guatemala.

This issue of controlling Latin America has been an obsession. The United States could develop a new sort of leadership in this hemisphere that even we could accept. This would not be based on attempts to control the internal organization of our countries but on mutual cooperation, mutual security, mutual prosperity.

Unbeknownst to most Americans, the United States still maintains a military facility in Cuba — the Guantánamo Naval Base. The United States imposed this base on Cuba as a condition for its independence in 1902, and then reaffirmed its rights to the base in a 1934 treaty that granted Guantánamo Bay to the United States in perpetuity. The revolutionary government has bitterly opposed this U.S. base and it is one of the obstacles standing in the way of normalizing relations. Why does the United States continue to hold on to the Guantánamo Base?

The base is a liability for the United States. It could easily be wiped out at the very beginning of any confrontation. Why should those Americans be placed there by their government like sitting ducks in a shooting gallery? And at a time when the United States is closing bases all over the world, why keep a base open that is all expenditure — everything from water to peanut butter has to be shipped in — but creates no jobs for the U.S. economy? I think it is because some people in the CIA or the Pentagon may want to use the base as a way to fabricate another Gulf of Tonkin incident in the future.

This issue of Guantánamo is a perfect example of the outdated premises on which U.S. policy is based. Perhaps in the last century there were some reasons for this type of a base. There were no missiles, there were no satellites, so it was important to have military bases everywhere. The United States needed coal to keep its ships running. It also needed access to markets and cheap labor. Therefore, a number of reasons existed, even if morally wrong, for wanting direct control. But in today's world, the idea of controlling a zone by having military bases is totally obsolete.

We are now at a time when global politics and the global economy don't work the way they did in the 19th century, or even the first half of the 20th century. The aims of the capitalist world — which is the only world that exists today — cannot be carried out with obsolete policies and instruments. This is not the time to find new answers to old questions, but to discover whether or not the questions themselves are properly posed. And certainly in the case of Cuba, the questions are improperly posed.

If the United States would have provided a different kind of leadership in this hemisphere many past conflicts might have been avoided. Also, we could avoid many other conflicts that might arise in the future if the United States would learn to develop a more constructive relationship with Latin America.

The restrictions that the U.S. government places on trade with Cuba are referred to in the United States as a trade embargo. But the Cubans refer to this as a blockade. Why?

The U.S. government and media use the term embargo, but an embargo would refer to a policy that affects only the United States and Cuba. The U.S. policy goes way beyond that. It is an extraterritorial policy that tries to impose itself on the rest of the planet. The United States uses all possible means — including U.S. embassies around the world — to monitor and track every trade and investment deal with Cuba. All business people who trade with Cuba are told that while they are free to do so, they may be exposing themselves to U.S. reprisals.

Recently, I met a Mexican who sells soap and toilet articles overseas. He had made a deal with Cuba to send two containers full of soap, a transaction worth about $40,000. Now remember that we are talking about soap — something you take showers with, not exactly what you could call a strategic commodity.

Well, soon after selling the soap to Cuba, this man was invited out for breakfast with a friend of his. At the breakfast was a man he didn't know, who turned about to be an official with the U.S. embassy in Mexico. This guy took out a bunch of documents and said very bluntly, "Look, we know that you recently sold some soap to Cuba for $40,000. And we also know that you've sold $1.5 million worth of goods to the United States. Now, you have all the right in the world to choose your friends, but you ought to choose your friends wisely and decide who is a better friend to have — the United States or Cuba."

There is still this kind of madness going around. In fact, it's worse now because I suppose there are lots of people in the CIA and the Pentagon who don't have a lot to do and are trying to justify their jobs. All the people and resources that had previously been concentrated on trying to overthrow the Soviet Union and Eastern Europe are now concentrated on Cuba. So I would definitely say that the U.S. policy of stopping others from trading with Cuba constitutes a blockade, not merely an embargo.

The United States has a history of using economic warfare to make countries "cry uncle." We did this to Chile under Allende, with the goal of "making the economy scream." In Nicaragua under the Sandinistas, we tried to make life for ordinary citizens so miserable that they would rise up against the government. Is this the same tactic being used against Cuba?

Exactly, it is a policy designed to make the daily life of Cubans miserable. The United States wants to make sure that when you wake up in the morning, there is no toothpaste to brush your teeth and no soap to take a shower. You try to make some breakfast and all you have is sugar water. You wait hours in the morning to get a bus to go to work, and there are so few buses you end up clinging on for dear life. You get to work and your workplace is closed because there is no electricity. You go through the same trauma to get home, and then you have to stand in line for hours to get food for your family.

This policy has meant that we can no longer give one liter of milk a day to all children under 13, as we used to do. Now we can only give it to children under 7 because we don't have enough for the rest. It has meant that cases of malnutrition have reappeared in a country that had achieved the best health record in all of Latin America during the past two decades.

It's a way to punish the Cuban population. It's a way to promote tension and anger against the system. When you don't have important medicines for a patient whose life is in danger, if you have to go without milk for the children, you're pushing the population into desperation. It reminds me of what the Nazis did with the Warsaw ghetto when they put the Jews together in one part of the city and threw bread to them so they could watch the people fight for it.

This is a war of attrition. I would certainly call it cruel and unusual punishment. If Cubans have not died in large numbers as a result of U.S. policy, it is due to the incredible effort on the part of the government to ensure equal distribution of scarce resources. Otherwise, we would be experiencing massive starvation.

The person who best described this policy is William Saffire a few years ago in the *New York Times* when he said that the Bush administration's policy toward Cuba was to make the Cuban people hungry enough so that they would get angry and over-throw their government. It's a crime to make the people of Cuba hungry. The U.S. blockade is not aimed at weakening the island's military capability. It's aimed at punishing the Cuban people for supporting their government. It's exactly this kind of policy that makes the Cuban people angry at the United States. If the United States were smarter, it would be trying to change the image it has acquired in Cuba over the last 100 years.

Is the United States still carrying out covert operations against Cuba?

U.S. policy is essentially based on the low-intensity conflict doctrine which was embraced by the Pentagon as a sort of rectification of the military doctrine of the Vietnam years. Since Vietnam, every time the United States wants to change a situation overseas through military means, it has applied this new doctrine, which tries its best to avoid the use of U.S. ground forces in any operation. This is the same kind of doctrine that was applied in

Nicaragua and El Salvador during the time of the Central American turmoil. They are now using the economic and psychological aspects of that doctrine. The military aspect would require U.S. ground troops. The air force can punish the enemy but cannot win a war, and the use of ground troops would be extremely costly in the case of Cuba.

So you would rule out a direct military invasion?

There was a time during the Reagan years, from about 1982-84, when this was a real possibility. But not so much since then. An invasion of Cuba would be particularly problematic. The Cuban defense system can impose a high casualty rate on any invading force. And that's why the Pentagon has applied mostly economic instruments in this low-intensity conflict. We can never rule out an invasion because we know the Pentagon has not ruled it out and regularly trains U.S. forces for that eventuality. But for the moment, they use other tools of war.

In addition to the economic war, the United States also uses psychological warfare. Radio and TV Martí are financed by the U.S. government to broadcast counterrevolutionary propaganda, and then there are some 15 private Miami stations broadcasting 24 hours a day.

The third tactic is to artificially create dissenting groups in Cuba to try to galvanize anger and tension and transform this tension into a political opposition to the government. But the United States recognizes that it has failed miserably in building up significant opposition groups on the island. There are a few small groups, but they have not been able to transform themselves into something like Solidarity in Poland. That failure is due to the very nature of the U.S.-Cuba conflict, in which Cubans see dissidents as being allied to a foreign power that has been the historical enemy of their nation. They do not view this as dissent against a particular form of government, but as an instrument of foreign aggression toward Cuba. In fact, that is why some people in Miami are in favor of lifting the blockade, for they think it would create a better environment for building dissent.

The Cuba Democracy Act, also known as the Torricelli bill after that congressperson who introduced it, was signed into law in October 1992. As you know, this law tightens restrictions on trade with Cuba by making it illegal for U.S. subsidiaries based in other countries to trade with Cuba. This subsidiary trade was previously an important source of foods and medicines for Cuba. The legislation also reduces aid to any nation that imports Cuban sugar and pressures U.S. allies not to trade with Cuba. Has this been effective?

The Torricelli Act has had many negative effects on Cuba. For example, there are complications in shipping goods to Cuba because it states that if a ship goes to Cuba, it cannot enter U.S. ports for another six months. This obviously discourages ships from stopping in Cuba.

Another negative effect is that the Treasury Department, the State Department and the CIA have been working harder to strengthen the blockade. I mentioned the story about the Mexican guy selling soap. This is a minor thing, but in other cases the United States has been successful in deterring important investments. There was a time, even before the Torricelli Act, when a Spanish company wanted to invest $150 million in the tourist development on an island off the coast of Cuba. The company had to back down from a contract that was already signed when it received a letter for the U.S. Treasury Department stating that U.S. markets would be closed to them if they went through with the investment.

When the Torricelli Act was proposed, it was stated this bill had both "carrots and sticks." Is there anything in the bill that you would consider a "carrot"?

I don't think there are any benefits in this bill for the Cuban people. The Torricelli Act spoke of better mail and phone service between the two countries as the carrots. The mail service is exactly the same as it was before the Act and we will not have normal mail service until the United States agrees to have regular commercial flights, not just charter flights, between Cuba and the

United States. The same with telephone service. The United States continues to freeze the bank account with the funds the U.S. telephone company owes us, and until that account is unfrozen, it will be difficult to improve the communications between the two countries. So I think these supposed carrots were just an excuse by the policy makers to try to present the legislation in a better light.

What has been the international reaction to the United States position on Cuba?

Other countries — the Mexicans, the Canadians — are rejecting the extraterritorial nature of the Torricelli Act, because it limits their sovereignty. The United States tried to blackmail them with the Free Trade Agreements, but these countries have stubbornly rejected the notion that the United States can dictate whom they can and can't trade with. The U.S. embargo was roundly condemned at the UN in November 1992 by a vote of 59 to 3, with only Israel and Romania supporting the U.S. position. It was also condemned in July 1993 by 23 Latin American heads of state.

But, again, the problem is that nowadays the CIA has very little work to do. With the demise of the Eastern bloc, a lot of people have to justify their salaries at the end of each month. Most of the personnel that were dealing with the Soviet bloc are now devoted to monitoring every single economic relationship that Cuba has. So while other governments condemn the embargo, it still acts as a deterrent for individuals and companies.

Do you have any figures on the amount of trade Cuba has lost because of the U.S. embargo?

The blockade has cost the Cuban economy about $40 billion since 1960. It has a tremendous impact on us, especially today. But I should also say that I think the blockade as such is an endangered species. It is already an obsolete weapon that has been repudiated worldwide. And the business community in the United States is, in increasing numbers, telling the U.S. government that it is a stupid strategy because by the time the embargo is lifted, it will be too late for the American business community to enter Cuba.

What do the United States and Cuban governments say must happen before they will enter into negotiations to normalize relations?

The Cuban agenda for normalizing relations with the United States has been very consistent. We have asked for an end to all aggression against our sovereignty, the withdrawal from the Guantánamo Base, and the lifting of the embargo. The U.S. agenda, on the other hand, has been a very slippery one. As soon as the goal posts are reached, then they move again.

At one time the United States said that in order to begin negotiations Cuban troops had to leave Angola, Cuba had to cease its involvement with revolutionary movements in Central America, and Cuba had to lessen its dependence on the Soviet Union.

Now that all of the issues have been dealt with, the U.S. agenda has completely changed and has moved from concern about our foreign affairs into the realm of our domestic, internal affairs. The U.S. government now says that before normalizing relations, Cuba must have a market economy, a multi-party system and Fidel Castro must leave power. My guess is that even if tomorrow we would have a market economy and a multi-party system, the United States would continue its hostility if we tried to maintain our sovereignty and independence from it.

I would even bet that if tomorrow some clown like Jorge Mas Canosa from Miami [president of the conservative Cuban American National Foundation] would become the president of Cuba, if he tried to maintain some shred of sovereignty, if he tried to have a nationalist economic policy, if he was not willing to become a servile ally, the same old story would prevail. Whatever concessions Cuba would make to the United States, whatever changes of structure, whatever changes in leadership, the conflict between the United States and Cuba will remain unless the United States is willing to give up the assumptions of the Monroe Doctrine.

So in my opinion it's not a question of a market economy or

the type of political system we have, it's a question of the hegemony that the United States wants to have over Latin America and, of course, wants to restore over Cuba.

Could you envision a change in U.S policy whereby the United States would lift the trade and travel restrictions and reestablish relations with Cuba as a way to subvert from within?

Sure. There is a big difference between normalizing relations and reestablishing relations. Normalization means that we can coexist and not try to subvert each other's reality. Canada is a good example of the kind of normal relationship the United States could have with Cuba. Canada is a capitalist society and does not particularly like the nature of the Cuban system. But Canada trades with Cuba, it has cultural exchanges with Cuba, and it is not trying to subvert the Cuban revolution.

Cuba has this kind of relationship with most capitalist countries, such as Japan, Sweden, France, and Germany. While none of these countries are particularly sympathetic toward Cuba's socialist regime, they have accepted that it is our right to determine the evolution of Cuban politics. So it is perfectly conceivable for a capitalist United States and a socialist Cuba to peacefully coexist, to have normal relations, if the United States were willing to accept Cuba's sovereignty.

On the other hand, the United States could very well reestablish relations with Cuba without normalizing them. This would be a way to keep the same policy goals — that of overthrowing the Cuban revolution — while changing the instruments of policy from hostility and blockade to a kind of friendly subversion. This is a tactic that a number of people in Miami are putting forward. Their idea is to coopt the country economically, politically, and ideologically by reestablishing relations.

It certainly makes sense from the U.S. point of view. If you have already tried every trick in the book and they have all failed, you might as well try friendly subversion.

Of course, Cuba's preference is to normalize relations. However, if this is not possible, we would prefer reestablishing relations over the present state of hostility. We prefer having a more civilized way of clashing. There would not be assassination attempts, bombings, starving people into submission, etc. Instead we would have the natural process that takes place when two different societies try to influence each other. In any case, it would be a step in the right direction. Also, we must remember that you can't normalize relations without first establishing relations.

This brings us to the issue of the Clinton administration and its policy toward Cuba. You are well aware that Clinton, during his presidential campaign, expressed support for the Torricelli Act even before George Bush did. In fact, Bush had problems with some of the trade restrictions in the bill, because it contradicted the U.S. position elsewhere on a "free market." But once Clinton backed it, Bush had no choice.

I see Clinton's support of the Torricelli Act as a campaign tactic to win the vote of the Cuban-American community in Florida. It doesn't mean that he sees the Act as a permanent instrument of foreign policy. Now that he is president, he can behave differently. The law leaves a number of its measures up to the discretion of the president, so he has the possibility of interpreting it in a more aggressive way or a more prudent way. Besides, laws are not written in stone. They can be changed, they can be reinterpreted.

We in Cuba see Clinton as trying to emulate John Kennedy by providing inspiration to the American people, particularly around domestic issues. But the Kennedy administration was contradictory, especially in foreign affairs. Kennedy created the Peace Corps to show the United States as extending a helping hand, and he also created the Green Berets. There is another point: administrations come and go, but bureaucracies remain, and these are bureaucracies that grew up in the Cold War era. All the same, I hope for the best.

Do you think it is possible that Clinton could risk alienating the Cuban-Americans and anti-Castro congress people and do

what Nixon did with China, saying "I'm going to be the one who is going to lead the way to normalizing relations with Cuba"? Is that possible?

First of all, Clinton does not risk "losing" the Cuban-American vote, because the majority did not vote for him anyway. I don't think that he'd go so far as to say he'd like to normalize relations with Cuba. He's more likely to say that the instruments used in the past to overthrow the revolution — that is, the blockade and continued hostility — did not succeed. Thus, being a pragmatic person, he could call for new instruments to bring about the same goal, including lifting some restrictions on travel and trade. I don't share Clinton's goals, but I would certainly welcome more ethical and humane instruments of conducting foreign policy.

On the other hand, there are forces in the United States that would love to put the Clinton administration on a collision course with Havana. They have been pressing Clinton to make statements condemning Cuba or to intensify U.S. hostility toward Cuba. These people have vested interests in the Cold War, vested interests in trying to maintain hostilities, and they are scared that Clinton might do something different.

We should also remember that there are forces in the United States that might play tricks to get Clinton in their camp. For example, during the Carter years there was a misinformation campaign by CIA officials to convince Carter that Cuba had promoted the invasion of Shaba in Zaire from Angola, when this was not the case. The CIA knew that this was a total distortion and manipulation of the facts. Their intention was to put the new Carter administration on a collision course with Cuba. So we might expect similar tricks now.

Who are these forces?

They are made up of the very same people who killed John F. Kennedy, the same people who have a vested interest in the Cold War. These people include Cold Warriors in federal agencies, together with fanatical right-wing Cuban-Americans.

What do you say to criticism about sounding like a conspiracy theorist?

Those people who don't believe in the conspiracy theory are going to have a hard time trying to convince people that every time a major political figure gets killed in the United States, a lunatic is behind it. Martin Luther King was chased and provoked by the FBI. It's hard to believe that then some wacko came with a rifle and killed him.

As a Cuban I have lived through many CIA conspiracies against my country. Those who refuse to see power struggles behind historical events are simply naive.

Given that Cuba could never be as large a trading partner as Russia and China, or even Vietnam for that matter, what does the United States have to gain by normalizing relations with Cuba?

The United States would gain stature internationally, because its policy is rejected by most governments in the world. This can be seen every time there is a secret ballot to elect Cuba at the United Nations. When countries can avoid reprisals and express their preferences, they overwhelmingly vote for us.

There would also be economic benefits from lifting the blockade. Cuba would buy hundreds of millions of dollars worth of U.S. goods, which would create more U.S. jobs. And when the United States finally lifts the restrictions on travel to Cuba, who is going to cash in on the $2-3 billion a year that American tourists will be spending? Will it be European and Latin American companies, or American ones?

Cuba also has developed a high-tech sector in biotechnology, which is the only one in the world with cheap labor. It has the possibility of significantly reducing the cost of medicines in the United States. The U.S. pharmaceutical industry could even make arrangements to use the research and development capacity or the production capacity of our labs. With the present U.S. necessity of lowering health care costs, this could be a positive factor.

A study by Johns Hopkins University said that in the first year or two after lifting the blockade, U.S.-Cuba trade could amount to about $2 billion a year. While this may not be very significant for the U.S. economy, it represents a huge portion of Cuba's trade, given that in 1992 Cuba had a purchasing power of only $2.2 billion. You sound like you're advocating going back to the pre-revolutionary situation, where the United States was by far Cuba's major trading partner.

Cuba's purchasing power in 1992 might have been $2.2 billion, but in 1989 it was over $8 billion. We hope that we will emerge from our present economic crisis and have a larger economy again. In any case, I'm not advocating that we go back to a dependence on the United States. We had that before the revolution and then we had the problem of dependence on the Soviets. We certainly don't want to go full swing backwards again.

In today's world, self-reliance is virtually impossible — even the United States is not self-reliant. But the only way to have some sort of economic independence is to multiply your dependencies by having a variety of trading partners. We want to strengthen our trade relations with all of Latin America, and with Japan, China, and Western Europe. But because of geographic proximity, it is logical for a major percentage of our trade to be with the United States. For example, we are presently importing rice from Vietnam, spending several times more in shipping than if we purchased rice from the United States. Before the revolution, by the way, we used to get our rice from Arkansas.

There's some irony in that!

Yes, maybe some farmer friends of Bill Clinton in Arkansas will have a message to send to the White House! Arkansas is a lot closer to Cuba than Vietnam, and both of us need the trade.

Migration and Miami

What is preventing a reassessment of U.S. policy towards Cuba? Is it primarily the conservative Cuban American lobby based in Miami?

The ultra-right wing of the Cuban American community in Miami, represented by Jorge Mas Canosa and the Cuban American National Foundation, has artificially built up a certain legitimacy and has captured center stage in Washington. They have been expressing themselves as the voice of the Cuban Americans, while in reality they represent a very vocal minority in that community.

But they are a minority that is well financed and well trained in lobbying in Washington. They have an incredible amount of resources and can get free publicity in many news media throughout the country.

I find it amazing the tactics that these fanatical people use, all in the name of bringing democracy to Cuba. They run Miami like Al Capone ran Chicago in the 1920s. They bomb and issue death threats against those members of the Cuban community who might not like the regime in Cuba, but are in favor of a re-establishment of relations with Cuba.

Don't you think that they are starting to lose credibility? There have been so many negative exposés on Mas Canosa and others of his ilk in the media starting in 1992. Even Americas Watch, which never reports on human rights issues in the United States, issued a report condemning the tactics used by right-wing Cuban Americans in Miami.

My sense is that the Cuban American National Foundation is losing support, even among conservatives in Washington. All of a sudden the media is paying attention to the terrorist tactics of the right wing community, to its lack of democratic attitudes. Many in Congress feel that it's time to hear a new voice.

How likely is that to happen, given the power of this conservative community?

I think many people, including President Clinton, have over-estimated the power of the right wing. The Clinton administration has two options. One is to submit to the current state of mind dictated by the right-wing Cuban community, and the other is to try to reshape public opinion. I think that many people in Florida might not like Fidel Castro and might not like how the regime is organized, but they are in favor of having more normal communication, more back and forth, and that's an agenda that Clinton could take up and get support on.

Every time the U.S. government has wanted to switch a policy toward Cuba, it has known how to play certain sectors against each other. It's like a stereo system with a left loud-speaker and a right loud-speaker and someone in the White House controls the balance. If they want to follow a right-wing policy, they turn the balance to the right speaker and you'll only hear in the media what the ultra-right is saying about U.S. policy toward Cuba. And when they want to change the policy, all of a sudden the loud-speaker of the left is turned up a little and you start hearing voices you never heard before that are advocating a warming of relations.

This happened when Jimmy Carter became president — all of a sudden people that nobody had heard of started to have a voice in the major media. So I don't necessarily believe that Washington is hostage to the Cuban American community. If they want to look into this community for more rational voices — even majority voices — they will find them.

People say that Clinton just doesn't want to deal with Cuba, certainly not during his first term. He has too many domestic issues on his plate and he has nothing to gain by changing the status quo vis-a-vis Cuba.

Clinton might not want to deal with Cuba, but the problem is that foreign affairs are not like frozen pizzas. You cannot put them in the freezer and take them out four years later. They have a dynamic of their own, they can get complicated the moment you least expect it. So whenever there is an opportunity to make a reassessment of policy, it's best to do that.

One of the constant sources of tension between the United States and Cuba has been around immigration. From the Cuban point of view, what have been the main problems?

In 1984, the State Department agreed to allow up to 20,000 Cubans a year to come to the United States as permanent residents. It was a good agreement that was worked out with the Reagan administration. But the United States didn't live up to that agreement. It interpreted it as meaning that they could allow from one person a year to 20,000 a year. And between 1984 and 1992, instead of granting visas to 160,000 Cubans, the United States had given visas to only about 8,000.

Thousands of people have permission from the Cuban government to leave, but no U.S. visas. So this creates a very difficult internal dynamic that forces people to leave in rafts, at great risk to their lives. It is a manipulative and cruel way for the United States to make Cuba look as if it is stopping people from leaving and forcing them to risk their lives on the high seas, when it is really the U.S. immigration policy. And these people who get to the United States through these very dramatic and risky methods are treated as heroes when they arrive, but people who want to travel through normal means and take a plane to Miami are denied their visas.

Even visas for temporary trips to the United States are often rejected on the grounds that the applicants may want to stay permanently in Miami. This hampers academic exchanges, cultural exchanges, all kinds of people-to-people ties. My own case is an example. When I was invited on a national speaking tour to the United States in 1993, I was given the visa literally 12 hours before I was supposed to get on the plane. It makes the planning of such trips extremely difficult.

The contradictions in U.S. immigration policy are quite astounding. On one hand, any Cuban who gets here, no matter how he or she arrives, is legally entitled to stay. On the other hand, the United States refuses to fill the immigration quota and tightens the blockade, thereby increasing scarcity in Cuba and creating a situation where more people want to leave the country.

The United States will either have to increase the number of legal visas, so people don't have to risk their lives coming in rafts, or lift the blockade so conditions in Cuba improve and those people are not forced to leave.

Another glaring contradiction in U.S. immigration policy is the treatment of Cubans versus the treatment of Haitians. Cubans who come to the United States illegally are given heroes' welcomes while Haitians are turned back to a country where their lives are truly in danger. I remember an incident where two Cubans were picked up at sea by a boatload of Haitian refugees, and when the U.S. coast guard stopped the boat, they welcomed the two Cubans to the United States and sent the Haitians back to sea.

Yes, the policy is certainly not a rational one. Look at this issue of restricting the rights of U.S. citizens to travel to Cuba. The U.S. government spends millions of taxpayer dollars a year to broadcast radio and TV propaganda to Cuba to convince Cubans of the glories of capitalism. But at the same time, you prevent U.S. tourists from visiting Cuba to influence the Cuban population by direct people-to-people contact — a type of "friendly subversion" that would not cost U.S. taxpayers a cent.

The U.S. government prevents Cubans from coming on temporary visits to see the marvels of the U.S. society and become converted to the American way of life. It prevents U.S. business people from going to Cuba to teach us capitalist management techniques. Where is the rationale behind all this?

But don't these restrictions cut both ways? Doesn't the Cuban government also restrict people who want to travel, even on temporary visits?

There was a time in which Cubans were restricted in their ability to visit and to migrate to other countries. This policy was reviewed and made more flexible, so that people who want to can leave and people can travel and come back. There are a number of artists, writers and sports figures who get jobs abroad for several years and then go back to Cuba. The major restriction on travel is Cuban pesos, which is not a currency that is convertible in the international market. You cannot go to a travel agency and pay for your ticket in pesos. So you have to have dollars or be invited by someone abroad — like a relative in Miami — who can pay for your ticket.

One of the tragic consequences of revolutions is how it divides families, how it creates such profound suffering among family members who end up on different sides of the fence. I know that some of this is the inevitable result of a revolution. We can see in Nicaragua, how within one family you have both leaders of the revolution and leaders of the opposition. Is there any way to heal some of the deep wounds within the Cuban community and work towards reconciliation.

With the fanatical right, this is impossible. But we must remember that people left Cuba for so many different reasons. Yes, some left because they disagreed with socialism, and they went to the United States to fight the revolution from there. But despite the media image, most people who migrated to the United States did not come for political reasons, especially since the 1970s. Most came looking for a better economic situation for themselves.

There has always been migration in the Caribbean to the United States. Mexicans who cross the border are not called political refugees; everyone knows they come to the United States for economic reasons. The same is true with most Cubans. The problem with Cubans is that once they get to Miami, they have to make a political statement against the revolution to get U.S. assistance and fit in with the tone in Miami. So the issue gets politicized. If they make the right statement they are automatically handed a green card for residence in the United States. Does any Haitian, Guatemalan, or Salvadoran ever have that privilege?

But there is an increasing awareness in Cuba that the

majority of the Cubans who migrated to the United States don't have a particularly hostile attitude toward the revolution. In 1978 a dialogue with this more moderate sector of the Cuban American community took place in Havana. But then came the Mariel boatlift in 1980, when over 100,000 Cubans migrated to the United States. U.S.-Cuban relations worsened, and the dialogue with the Cuban-American community was cut off.

The future and revolution

Do you think there is a possibility that the United States, in this post-Cold War era, will reassess its policies toward Latin America in general?

Objectively speaking, the world has changed and it is certainly time for a sweeping reassessment of U.S. policy. It is time for U.S. policymakers to leave the bipolar world behind and start to understand the complexity of this new era we are entering.

Latin America can no longer be seen primarily as a source of cheap labor and raw materials. First of all, with today's new technologies, the need for cheap labor and materials is less critical. With the emergence of the multinational corporations, flexible technologies and synthetic raw materials have replaced the need for large labor reserves and for many Third World commodities as well.

More important is the issue of markets for U.S. goods. In terms of markets, trade with Latin America as compared to U.S. trade with the First World has been declining consistently. The United States needs more markets for its products, but Latin America is too impoverished to buy significant amounts of these goods. It would therefore help the United States economy — as well as the economies of Latin America — to have policies that raise the standard of living of the workers in Latin America, rather than a policy of exploiting cheap labor. There are some 400 million people in Latin America. If living conditions were upgraded, Latin America would become an incredible market for the United States.

How do you think the free trade agreement between the United States, Canada and Mexico — and potentially with many other Latin American countries — would affect the economies of Latin America?

This would mainly benefit the major corporations, those in a better position to be competitive, and would hurt medium and small-sized businesses. For example, most of the investment we are receiving in Cuba from Latin America and even Europe is precisely from medium or small-sized businesses, because they are trying to escape the impact of free trade agreements in Europe and Latin America. Many Mexicans who feel they will not be able to survive the free trade agreements are trying to diversify.

So I believe we're going to have a global economy that will be structured along the lines of major transnational corporations. That will bring about more polarization of power, bankrupting thousands and thousands of medium and small-scale entrepreneurs. They will enter the growing pool of workers without jobs.

The demise of the Soviet Union has led to a new world order, but is there anything in this new order that will benefit the Third World?

This new order will not transform itself into a rose garden but into a nightmare if certain tendencies are not changed. If the world continues to be one of the powerful exploiting the powerless, if it continues to become more and more polarized in terms of the have and the have nots, then we will be witnessing massive upheavals in the future.

There are now more objective conditions for revolution than there were when Che Guevara went to fight in Bolivia. But it seems that in the immediate future, there will be social upheavals but not revolutions, because there seems to be no viable model at this point.

Let me use an image of Trotsky: Revolutions are like the piston of an engine. If there is a lot of steam in the engine but no pistons on them, all the steam will evaporate and there will be no direction, no forward motion. With the fall of the Soviet Union, the left is so confused and demoralized. It lacks new viable programs that could turn social explosions, which is the undirected steam that comes out of the engine, into revolutions.

We have witnessed that steam, those social explosions, in Venezuela, in Argentina, in Brazil, in the Domincian Republic, and, oh yes, in Los Angeles. And I'm just referring to the Western hemisphere, for there are plenty of similar tensions boiling in other parts of the world as well.

Do you think there is a possibility that Latin America will come together in its own free trade zone as a way to counter the power of the United States?

We might well witness a new emergence of Latin American alliances in the next 5-10 years. We cannot continue forever with the erosion of the terms of trade that the southern countries have experienced since the 1980s and the increased level of poverty. Take even the most touted economy in Latin America — Chile — and you'll find that on the macro-economic level, inflation has been curbed, exports have increased, the GNP is growing. But more than half of the population has been pushed below the poverty level.

That kind of polarization between the rich and poor in the name of neo-liberal policies and the international market is going to bring about more social tensions in these countries. And these social tensions are going to convert themselves into more pressure on national governments to enter into collective agreements with other Latin American countries for better terms of trade with the north.

How do you think the majority of Americans feel about Cuba?

I don't know. I was discouraged when I recently met a professor from a major U.S. university and he said that when he asked his students where Cuba was, they thought it was close to China.

I don't think that is typical — at least I hope not. But the surveys do say that the majority of American people, if they read the newspaper, prefer sports and comics to political news. So I don't think they know too much about Cuba.

They probably have certain images, certain flashes that they see on TV between one commercial and another saying that Fidel Castro is a dictator. There are certain words that are always linked to Cuba. Dictatorship. Repression. Chaos. Economic decline. You don't get any kind of in-depth analysis but quick encapsulated snapshots using pejorative buzzwords.

Like communism.

Yes, like communism, which in the United States is still like mentioning Satan. So the view that is portrayed is that Cuba is an enemy of the United States, that it is dangerous, but that it is also collapsing and will disappear any day now.

There must be many people who are asking themselves why it hasn't disappeared already, since for a long time Cuba was described as a satellite of the Soviet Union. Well, if the Soviet planet is gone, how come the satellite is still circling?

What is your opinion of the American people?

I have great respect for the American people. I know Americans very well. I went to an American school, I worked as a diplomat in the United States, I was even married to an American. I feel certain that if the American people had a better understanding of Cuban reality, even if they reject the notion of communism and the policies of the Cuban government, even if they would like to see an end to socialism, they would still be in favor of a more ethical policy towards Cuba. They would prefer to bring about change in Cuba by exposing Cubans to the influence of Americans and not by trying to annihilate the Cuban people with a war of attrition.

What's been the role of international solidarity in terms of helping the Cuban people during this economic crisis?

In terms of solidarity, there has been a growing movement all around the world. Even people who are from poor, under-developed countries like India, for example, have been making an incredible effort to send food and medicines to Cuba. We have been receiving support from solidarity groups throughout the world.

In the United States, there are a number of groups giving humanitarian aid and solidarity to the Cuban population. I find it remarkable that there are even people in the Cuban-American community in Miami who have been helping us with significant contributions. I have great respect for that effort, because I know that some of the people who are engaged in it do not necessarily sympathize with the government in Cuba. I also know that they have had to defy the ultra-right wing in Miami, who in the most insensitive way has refused to help the Cuban population. They prefer to keep their ideological purity and watch their own families on the island suffer.

Much of your work, and our work in the United States, is geared toward relieving tensions between the United States and Cuba and lifting the blockade. I must admit that I sometimes get this uncertain feeling that lifting the blockade would really spell the end of the revolution. With an influx of U.S. tourists and businesses, an influx of the consumer society, could the ideals of the revolution withstand such an onslaught? Do you have these same fears? Do you sometimes think that the opponents of the revolution who advocate reestablishing relations as a more efficient way to overthrow the revolution might be right?

They might well be. The revolution has gone through 35 years of hostility, but we haven't gone through one year of peace. We are accustomed to direct U.S. subversion. We are trained to resist aggression, we have built miles of tunnels and thousands of trenches. And not only are we trained to resist aggression but we have proven our efficiency in this struggle. So we're in all likelihood better equipped to handle an invasion by the 82nd Airborne Division than an ideological and cultural invasion.

If the U.S. administration were to switch to "friendly

subversion," we would be confronting a new terrain. Are we as prepared as we are for direct confrontation? I'd say no. Does this mean that we could not survive? No, not necessarily. But we will be better able to survive if we are capable of understanding this danger right now and don't wait until this change happens to then try to adapt ourselves ideologically and culturally to this new situation.

How could you get ready now for such an onslaught?

A policy of political and cultural co-optation is a much more complex policy, and is therefore harder to fight. It tries to confuse the population ideologically, it tries to subvert language and concepts. So an essential ingredient in fighting such co-optation is to decipher the codes.

What are some of these codes?

When the counterrevolutionary message speaks of "freedom," it is referring to free enterprise. When the counterrevolutionary message speaks of "democracy," it is referring to reestablishing political competition between powerful sectors. When the counter-revolutionary message speaks of "equality," it is referring to the re-establishment of juridical equality within a structure that is divorced from economic opportunities. When the United States speaks to us of a "new world order," it is speaking of the acceptance by Cuba of a transnational power, with its head-quarters in Washington.

These code words are accompanied by other ideological messages. One of them is that humanitarian utopias are not viable, that there is no alternative to capitalism. It says that capitalism has proven itself to be the only viable society and therefore we should concern ourselves with improving the capitalist system and not with building an alternative system.

Another message is that life only has meaning for each of us as individuals, and only in the present. We should not search for meaning in life in relation to the future or in relation to others, for life only has meaning for me and for now.

A related message is that in society, as in nature, the fittest survive. So the misfortune of others is not my problem and is not within my ability to solve. If people are poor, that is because they have lost out in the social competition and the only thing I can do is to guarantee my future and not try to establish a sense of solidarity with my neighbors.

A corollary concept, taken to a national level, is that history, the nation and even my life have no historical and ideological mission to fulfill. We are on this planet to live as individuals and neither my nation, nor history, nor I as an individual have a meaning or an objective other than the search for success, and success as defined as power over others.

And the ultimate message, which is logically tied to the others, is that I can be successful if I try hard enough. As the saying goes, "You can make it if you really try."

In the last analysis, the message is one of selfishness, immediacy and egotism — surely the antithesis of revolutionary values and ideals.

This conflict in the terrain of ideology, while it might indicate a new stage of the struggle in the "trenches of ideas," would really be a throwback to the conflicting ethical values that have put the United States and Cuba on a collision course for over 100 years. Isn't that so?

Yes, we are part of an historical movement of the ethic of being against the ethic of having. We are part of a movement that believes that human happiness does not reside in our unlimited capacity to consume but in our unlimited capacity to give solidarity to our fellow human beings. We are part of a tradition that believes that people have a mission to accomplish on earth, which is not the search for individual success but the search for the humanity we carry within us. In this way our existence forms part of a continuous historical thread and the path to immortality is to be part of this historic mission.

Our heroes are people like Martí and Che Guevara, those who gave their lives for their ideals, who transcended their personal existence by putting it in the service of the collective.

U.S. heroes, on the other hand, would be more like Rockefeller or Dupont or J.P. Morgan, or in today's world Lee Iacocca or Donald Trump. They would be the great businessmen who made your country, those who achieved personal success in a social jungle in which the Darwinist principles of the survival of the fittest is accepted as a valid social code. That is why I call the ideological conflict between the two countries as the ethic of being versus the ethic of having, and yes, this conflict has been raging for over a century.

What do you say to those who call you a dreamer, to those who might hold similar beliefs deep down but say you'll never win, so why keep up the fight?

In the best tradition of our Cuban revolutionary thought, there is clearly the notion that people make history. Instead of seeing inexorable laws of history, instead of believing that history inexorably led to a certain outcome, we see history as an ethical commitment and a human possibility. Martí, who died without achieving his goals, taught us that people make history not according to their real possibility of victory but according to their ethical commitment to justice. These are essential elements for understanding the evolution of our revolutionary process.

According to capitalist thinkers, yes, we are crazy people swimming against the tide of history. Socialism will inevitably fall everywhere and the Cuban revolutionary mission is therefore an anachronism — an anachronism that corresponds to a romantic, modern era that is being overtaken by a postmodern era. We can answer that the true Christians, not those of the Inquisition but those who have been fighting for a particular ethical code, have also been swimming against the tide of history for some 2,000 years!

Humanism, the human sense of existence, transcends the Cuban revolution; it transcends José Martí or Fidel Castro. The human character has two basic tendencies: egoism and altruism. Egoism embodies the ethic of "having," that I am worth a million dollars because I have a million dollars. Altruism embodies the ethic of "being," that I am worth what I am, as a measure of my virtues and defects.

The question is not whether or not the ethic of being can win out over the ethic of having. José Martí didn't believe that he would necessarily achieve victory in his lifetime, or that victory was even necessarily achievable. If we lose, as Martí did during the independence struggle, each defeat is accepted as a temporary setback, and we search for a strategic victory beyond the lifetime of the generation that is currently carrying out the struggle.

So it's not about winning, it's about taking a moral stand. We have to prove to ourselves and posterity that we were truly willing, in the words of Martí, to cast our fate with the poor of the earth. If we are not successful, perhaps the next generation will be.

CUBA:
"Socialist museum"
or social laboratory?

CUBA:
"Socialist museum" or social laboratory?
(Letter to a foreign friend)

CUBA IN "VIRTUAL REALITY"

Most of the "information" about Cuba which reaches world public opinion is composed and transmitted by transnational corporations, standardized with media buzz words, such as "economic crisis," "violation of human rights," "totalitarianism," and trivialized in its focus. Nevertheless, even if one were able to have access in other countries to alternative and diverse sources of information that avoided clichés and approached the Cuban reality in a deeper and more objective way, the question would remain the same: apart from being a possible place for beach vacations, why should Cuba be of interest to, for example, an Australian, a Canadian or a European? In what other way could the destiny of this small island of 12 million inhabitants affect such a person?

Cuba has gone through a crisis — perhaps more than one — and must make a radical transition in order to survive. This is true. But it is also true that all of humankind and its fragile spaceship Earth are facing a similar crisis (or several crises) that will force it, if it wishes to survive, to make radical changes of a global nature.

If Cuba is relevant to Australians, Canadians or Europeans, it is certainly not because of its dark-skinned beauties in swimsuits, its markets or its investment possibilities. Rather it is because this island possibly has something new to say about the model for sustainable human development that is urgently needed by the ecosystem and humanity at the end of the second millennium.

If Cuba were only an exotic museum of a dying "socialism," it would have little to say to a developed and now troubled capitalist world. However, if one can find in Cuba some of the pieces of the puzzle that constitute a model for alternative development, then our little island may again capture the attention of the developed north.

The transnational news agencies, such as AP, UPI, Reuters and AFP which provide 90 percent of all the international news that is published in the entire world, tend to concentrate on the museum-type aspects of the Cuban reality. Even this they distort, while they ignore other aspects that reflect the potential and promise of a revolutionary process that has succeeded in surviving the blows of its powerful neighbor and its own errors. Thus foreigners are denied access to the Cuban reality, which is replaced in the media by a delightful "virtual reality."

Today Cuba is, certainly, both a museum and a promise. It lives in the shadow of U.S. hostility and the country's own deeply rooted dogmas, but, despite the global financial and commercial blockade imposed by its powerful neighbor, it is fighting once more to break through the barriers that stand in the way of its future.

Cubans live in an unsatisfactory present, which is still highly superior to the way they used to live 35 years ago and also superior to the Latin American "democratic" reality beyond Cuba's shores today. If we were to use present conditions as a basis to defend ourselves against those forces that wish to restore the past we would be fighting a losing battle. Only by once again advancing can we avoid being trapped by the past. But, advancing where? Making a transition toward what?

NATION AND SOCIALISM
The history of the Cuban nation has been influenced by a number of peculiar and highly unusual factors.

The first feelings of national identity and their conceptual expression emerged in our incipient native-born oligarchy toward the end of the 18th century and the beginning of the 19th under the influence of European modernism. To "modernize" the island at that time meant to increase the efficiency of the slave plantations, to improve the infrastructure, to introduce new technology for production and services, to compete in the developing world market (both European and American, in this case) and to transform the system of education. Given their colonial situation, this socioeconomic program required a minimum of sympathy toward their project within the limited and ephemeral context of the enlightened despotism with which the Spanish Crown was experimenting in those years. Advancing the ideas of free enterprise, free commerce (forbidden by the Crown), political and civil liberties (except for slaves and the lower classes), obtaining representation in the Spanish Parliament and a minimum of administrative decentralization to achieve a degree of local autonomy — all these things formed part of the reformist project for the emergence of the nation. This nation was to have its roots in a utilitarian and pragmatic ethic, reflecting the bourgeois intellectual leadership in Europe and the United States of those times.

After several decades of whispering these ideas in ballrooms, theaters and mansions and sending them with due respect to the unmovable Spanish Parliament, our incipient oligarchy, which had already experimented successfully with some economic reforms, saw its proposals frustrated by the intolerance of a new, more despotic and less enlightened monarchy. With Latin America having attained its independence already, thus leaving "the loyal island of Cuba" alone in its colonial status, a new wave of ideas — this time revolutionary in nature — swept through the population.

Due to its utilitarian and pragmatic point of view, the most prosperous sector of the native oligarchy decided to postpone its nationalist project in the short run in order not to suffer further from Spanish intolerance. Others, a good number of whom had been reduced to middle-class status by now, enthusiastically embraced the nationalist program and organized the first Cuban war of independence in 1868. The first revolutionary act of the man who initiated that struggle, Carlos Manuel de Céspedes, was to liberate his slaves so that they could decide for themselves as free men and women whether as good "Cubans" they would accompany him, now as a leader and not as a master, to fight and die "for Cuba." When Céspedes tolled his bell in that dawn of October 10, 1868, to liberate a handful of slaves whose freely taken option for the struggle for independence suddenly transformed them into "Cubans," he was planting the seed for an alternative project of nationhood to that other utilitarian, reformist and pragmatic program which had failed in the face of Spanish intransigence. Nevertheless, tactical and programmatic differences within the leadership caused conflicts and divisions which, together with Spanish military superiority, led to the failure of this attempt at liberation after 10 cruel years of war.

Interestingly, it was a black leader who had risen to the rank of general in this war, Antonio Maceo, who, in a historic protest and without the means or reasonable possibility of continuing the struggle, refused to adhere to the armistice. He would be forced by reality to lay down his arms and go into exile with his collaborators, but only — together with many others — to prepare a new war and continue the people's revolutionary process.

A new anticolonial war of independence began on February 24, 1895, this time led by figures who emerged from the middle and lower classes, many of whom had seen action in the previous conflict. A young intellectual, a brilliant orator and exceptionally fine strategic thinker was to be the architect of the new struggle. José Martí, who lacked the fame and glory of the patriot generals and whose soft hands were more accustomed to wielding the pen than a machete or a rifle, would assemble a new army of liberation. He won respect from arrogant heroes, conceived the political program of the revolution and the future republic, forged a party capable of leading the struggle, subordinated military to civilian leadership and provided a social vision of the future.

This time the project of nationhood would not just be an alternative to colonial domination, but also an alternative to the newly independent Latin American republics already mired in social inequality and authoritarianism. The rebel nation, represented in these new insurrectionists, was now also the bearer of an *ethical* project for a Republic as defined by Martí. The man who had already declared, "I wish to cast my luck with the poor of the Earth," had conceived of a future Republic "with all and for the good of all."

Independence and social justice, since that time, have been the two central values in the formation of the cultural identity of the Cuban nation and defined the utopia which was frustrated by U.S. intervention in 1898 and its subsequent hegemony and domination on the island until January 1, 1959.

The native oligarchy, guided by its usual utilitarian and pragmatic approach to Cuban nationhood, took a peripheral role in local power and far from "developing" the Republic, made it an appendage of U.S. economics and politics.

Half a century of republican history on the periphery of capitalism and the frustration of several reformist and revolutionary movements persuaded the nation that only a radical transformation of the internal and external structures of Cuban capitalism, inspired by Martí's ideas, would open the way to the possibility of achieving the independent and just Republic to which it aspired.

The 1959 revolution, therefore, declared from the very beginning its intention to carry out profound structural changes and expressed the desire that the United States should understand and respect the inescapable necessity — and even desirability — of these changes. Nevertheless, in 1959 Washington did not show much more tolerance than the Spanish Crown had shown in the middle of the 19th century.

Fidel Castro definitively proclaimed the socialist nature of the revolution while enemy warships were approaching the Bay of Pigs in 1961. By doing so, he simply gave a name to the reality of the intense ideological process of radicalization, propelled by the recent radical structural changes and by the hostility the United States had demonstrated during the preceding two years.

In his time, José Martí had asked himself what kind of republic he wanted. Fidel Castro would now have to ask himself what kind of socialism he wished to build. If Martí's republican project was an alternative to both the colonial system and the injustices of Latin American societies, the Cuban socialist project would also have to become an alternative, not only to capitalism but also to the so-called European model of "actually existing socialism," the defects of which were already visible at that time, causing Che Guevara to foresee its generalized crisis three decades in advance.

Only a humanistic and democratic definition would connect Cuban socialism to its own ideological tradition and the national project. In the historical conditions prevailing in 1961 and in the face of U.S. intransigence, socialism would be the *only* viable option to achieve independence with social justice. For socialism to be legitimate in Cuba, it had to be built on the humanistic and democratic ideological framework provided by Martí. It would have to be politically, economically and socially "with all and for the good of all." It would have to guarantee the "freedom with bread and bread without terror" promised by Fidel Castro at the hour of victory. But Soviet socialism failed to bring these things together. Now advancing along the socialist path, Martí's model had no connection with the "actually existing socialist" world. It was therefore necessary to proceed by force of faith, imagination and wisdom in a world in which survival meant walking a geopolitical tightrope.

In contrast to Eastern Europe, where "socialism" arrived on the treads of Soviet tanks and, once the rejoicing and gratitude for liberation from the Nazi yoke had passed, it frequently clashed with local nationalist sentiments, in Cuba socialism was proclaimed by an armed populace about to go to the beaches of the Bay of Pigs to face the imperial invasion. The nation had decided, in the most dramatic way, that it was only through the socialist option that it was possible to achieve the Republic with independence and social justice for which it had fought for nearly a century. Nationhood, independence and social justice would now strive for historic viability along the socialist path.

SOCIALIST PLURALISM AND COHABITATION

But in the ranks of the revolution, made up of diverse ideological tendencies, there were different socialist criteria and visions which frequently clashed with each other. While everyone was revolutionary, not everyone understood Marxism and socialism in the same way and there were also some who opposed them.

People who had learned to admire the Soviet achievement of transforming the most backward country in Europe into a superpower in spite of a blockade, civil war and the Nazi invasion tended to dismiss and discredit as "anticommunist" or "anti-Soviet" any critical appraisal of life in the Soviet Union or in the countries of Eastern Europe. The notion of building a "different" socialism sounded heretical and "antiscientific" to them, at the very least. While the United States was now attempting to massively drain our small country of talent by providing professionals with inducements to emigrate, others believed that we should learn the ABCs of public and corporate management to survive the recently imposed U.S. blockade and also create, in a theoretical and practical way, a model of socialist development which would be an alternative to that prevailing in Eastern Europe.

Fidel Castro and Ernesto Guevara, with the audacity of authentic revolutionaries in the midst of difficult debates and struggles, ensured that the latter option prevailed in one way or another for the better part of the first decade of the Cuban socialist experiment. Central Marxist concepts such as the political participation of the masses, the questioning of the law of value as the main regulator of growth and development, internationalism and the promotion of an ethic based on solidarity were dusted off. Thus a creative and revolutionary understanding of socialism and Marxism overrode the "orthodoxy" of those who warned against "adventures" and "experiments" of an "idealistic" or "subjective" nature.

The tumultuous and radical decade of the 1960s served as the backdrop to the heresy of the young Cuban revolutionaries who, in their audacity and inexperience, were confident of triumph, despite not only the counterrevolutionary and imperialist challenge, but also the lack of understanding and intellectual intolerance of the well-ensconced bureaucratic elites of Eastern Europe. Che's death in Bolivia in 1967, the failure to achieve the 10-million-ton sugar harvest hoped for in 1969-70, the internal inflationary process which resulted from the abolition of all private services and production (with the exception of small farmers, who were also forced to sell their produce to the State at that time), combined with the general lack of adequate fiscal control encouraged by a hasty and poorly applied anti-bureaucratic campaign, brought about the crisis of the Cuban socialist vision and project.

With the Latin American revolutionary movement in retreat and nationalist military governments arising in the region, the Vietnamization of the conflict in Southeast Asia and the demobilization of the radical movement and the left after Prague Spring, Cuba was left with only two choices: to become another isolated Albania 90 miles from the United States, with a North American military base (Guantánamo) on its own territory, or strike — de facto, if not de jure — a "new deal" with the Soviet Union that would recognize the island's independence and autonomy and would also provide it with exceptional and advantageous commercial, financial and military accords, in exchange for greater orthodoxy in the methods and concepts of socialist construction.

The audacious attempt to "take heaven by storm" yielded to a relative, tropical-style "Russification" of the country's institutions, concepts and style. There was much back-patting in those years by the people who — inside and outside of Cuba — had warned against the "subjective" nature of Castroism (or *Fidelismo*, as it is known in Cuban terms). Everything, from now on — especially after the First Congress of the Cuban Communist Party in 1975 and for a decade and a half thereafter — would be done in a "scientific," "materialist" and "dialectical" fashion — that is, as in the Soviet Union.

The fact that these shifts in domestic and foreign policy were not accompanied — as they were in the Soviet Union or China — by serious repression and abuse of power against those whose perceptions and policies had prevailed up until that point speaks well of our revolutionary leadership, and especially that of Fidel Castro. Both currents of socialist thought achieved a difficult, uncomfortable but successful cohabitation with clear and narrow limits on their expression.

In spite of efforts here and there to give it a "tropical" flavor, the imported Soviet model and its supposedly "socialist" ethical code did not mesh well with Martí's democratic and humanist vision of independence and social justice in a republic "with all and for the good of all." Marxist ideology itself, wounded and traumatized by the difficult and heartrending Russian experience, was hardly recognizable in the alien creature which an adverse history brought forth under the name of "actually existing socialism."

From that point on, the Cuban revolutionary process and its socialist project would have to face not only U.S. aggression but also the mortal danger — as happened to the Leninist project in the Soviet Union — of being diverted onto the labyrinthine paths of bureaucratic state socialism. If the United States threatened the nation's very survival, the imported Soviet model threatened the survival of the revolutionary nature of the Cuban process and also, in the long run, endangered the survival of a nation which, if its political power were corrupted bureaucratically, would no longer be able to sustain its independence and social justice against the U.S. threat.

Little by little "the experience" of European socialism was transplanted into Cuba: bureaucratic planning, vertical administration, intellectual intolerance, the bureaucratization of civil society, etc. Again it would be Fidel Castro's personal role which — with due respect to the pro-Soviet consensus and spirit prevailing among most of the political leadership and the general population — would set limits to the pernicious influence of this schema of bureaucratic polarization between the leaders and the led, the underestimation of all criteria of the ethic of solidarity (national or international), the accommodation of technocratic elites and other evils that threatened to create a future political morass.

"There are things which are legal, but not moral," was a shot Fidel Castro fired while addressing a disconcerted youth congress in 1982, whose members were not likely to have known the background of such a statement, and even less likely to have understood its full meaning.

European "actually existing socialism" had already been diverted from its original course for too long to have been able to represent a true alternative to capitalism, with which it shared — in spite of notable differences — a hidden set of assumptions characteristic of modern industrial civilization. To dominate nature, to control society, to organize bureaucratic hierarchies in pyramidal style, mass production, centralization of power, the cult of statistics and "scientific" truths — these were all assumptions shared by industrial cultures in both East and West, while they also shared the criterion of economic cost-efficiency that excluded any analysis of the ecological and social impact of the development of production. That so-called "socialism" had already broken completely with Marxist ideals in order to construct another culture based on class domination, although with a more humanitarian and just sense of the distribution of goods and services lacking in its capitalist counterpart, which entrusted this function to the blind operation of market forces.

"I am not interested in socialism without communist morality," Guevara observed to Jean Daniel in 1963. "We are not only struggling against poverty, but also against alienation.... If socialism neglects the fact of conscience, it may be a method of distribution, but it will cease to be a revolutionary morality." It would be Guevara himself who would comment in an unpublished manuscript that "Stalin's tremendous historical crime" was "to have neglected communist education and to have instituted the unlimited cult of authority."

While Castro's and Guevara's vision of socialism emphasized an ethic of being — "I am worth the extent that my virtues and defects are in balance" — the Soviet model promoted an ethic of "having" — "I am worth according to what I have and own" — similar to that which prevails in capitalist societies. The "unlimited cult of authority" made bureaucratic upward mobility and the external symbols of hierarchical power, expressed in possessions and privileges, the ethical leitmotif of "actually existing socialism."

When parents educated their children they were more concerned with the professional quality of their instruction and their willingness to submit to the blind discipline of any higher authority, than with making them virtuous and decent human beings. The cult of deference to one's hierarchical superior implies the false supposition that all authority is always competent and moral, thus reproducing and sustaining the bureaucracy's social legitimacy. The "higher" one rose, the more one was considered to be not only "more competent" but also "a better person."

Cuban military and civilian internationalist missions in the 1970s and 1980s in Africa and Latin America, together with the humanist and democratic roots of Martí's philosophy and the socialist vision of Fidel Castro and Ernesto Guevara in which an entire generation had been educated throughout the decade of the 1960s, kept the Soviet model from completely destroying the revolutionary nature of the Cuban process, although it did bind the nation and the revolution in a conceptual strait jacket from which they have still not been able to completely break free. The Soviet model and its dogmatic interpretation of Marxism have been crumbling in Cuba since the middle of the last decade, but not all of its edifices have collapsed yet, and its ruins have not yet been removed.

In April of 1986, it would again be Fidel Castro who would make an appeal to open a process of national "rectification" to correct the "errors and negative tendencies" originating in the "mimetic excesses" incurred with regard to the Soviet model. In a way, that rectification process had begun two years earlier, when, aware of the fact that the Soviet Union would not become involved in a conflict with the United States in order to defend Cuba against Reagan's aggressive intentions, the Cuban leadership decided to make a radical shift from the conventional Soviet doctrine of defense to the doctrine of "a war of the entire people" in the eventuality of foreign intervention. This was not simply a technical military question. The new doctrine meant a return to original principles, using today's resources and experience: to train, arm and organize the entire population, to teach people how to make homemade weapons, to decentralize arsenals and place arms in the hands of people's militias based in factories, farms and universities. As Carlos Andrés Pérez, Menem or Balaguer could well understand such a concept presupposes a high degree of legitimacy and social consensus in favor of the government, without which it would not have been possible.

Between 1986 and 1991 a torrent of isolated and unconnected criticism rained on the mimicry of yesteryear from speaker's platforms, newspapers, classrooms and other places. Nevertheless, aside from the positive correction of a whole series of policies, no new comprehensive model for socialist development to replace the Soviet one was proposed. On this occasion there were no internal schisms, nor, in contrast to what had occurred in the early 1970s, were members of the executive team requested to turn in their resignations due to the simple fact that they had implemented previous policies according to criteria which were now being revised.

As a result of the disappearance of the Soviet Union in 1991, Cuba was launched into the so-called "special period in peacetime" which, translated from the military jargon in which the concept originated, implies the adoption of methods of wartime economy to deal with the immense impact which this event had had on the island: the sudden loss of 85 percent of its markets and virtually all sources of credit or technology, at the same time that the United States in 1992 gave another turn to the screw of the economic blockade with the Torricelli Act, in an opportunistic attempt to force Cubans, once and for all, to capitulate. The design of an alternative model of development — the strategic objective of the rectification campaign — was again subordinated to the struggle for the most basic survival which the new crisis demanded.

CONJUNCTURAL CRISIS AND STRUCTURAL CRISIS

Because of all the factors cited above, today Cuba is living through two parallel crises. One is of a structural nature, identified prior to the beginning of perestroika with the exhaustion of the development model imported from the Soviet Union. This fact led the political leadership to increasingly distance itself from that model until another model could be designed which would not only be as "effective," but which would be an authentic alternative, not only to "actually existing socialism" but also to capitalism. The response given to that structural crisis was the "rectification process" initiated at the beginning of the last decade.

The other crisis is of a conjunctural nature and has its origin in external factors: the collapse of the Eastern bloc and the intensification and extraterritorial extension of the U.S. blockade under these circumstances. The essence of this crisis is the necessity for international economic reintegration into markets and the need for sources of technology and capital for the country as a result of the new situation. The response to the conjunctural crisis has been the whole body of emergency measures adopted in the context of the so-called "special period in peacetime."

Of course, both crises are indissolubly connected, and their solution is to be found in overcoming the two forms of blockade: the U.S. blockade, with respect to the conjunctural crisis, and the blockade created by dogmatism, in relation to the structural crisis.

If the United States does not lift its blockade and extraterritorial pressures, Cuba will not have sufficient access to the markets and sources of financial credit and technology needed to successfully undertake the general restructuring of its development model. On the other hand, to confront the conjunctural crisis exclusively with those ad hoc measures that reality has imposed on us, without employing them in a coherent organizational framework that is not simply the general determination to avoid economic shock therapy for the population, could provoke the lethal equivalent which chemotherapy can have on cancer patients who submit to it in the hope of a cure. A thorough examination of the causes of the collapse of the Eastern bloc, with the exception of the modest and limited research of a few academics, is still awaiting the "opportune" moment — a moment which has already been delayed beyond all reason. Without that "autopsy," the task of formulating a new development model is complicated still further.

What Cuba is attempting now is an exceptional feat under the worst possible conditions: to construct a mode of production that is oriented toward the ordinary citizen's quality of life and provides just and equitable access to basic human necessities, at the same time as permitting internal space for productive and commercial transactions based on market principles contained in and regulated by state jurisprudence. Such an exceptional mode of production would in turn have to be integrated in a competitive fashion into the global economic system that functions on ruthless neoliberal principles of marketing and competition.

In brief, Cuba wishes to preserve and develop a code of humanist social ethics in its internal operations at the same time that it is forced to integrate itself into a global economic system that operates on strict principles of social Darwinism.

Cuba won't have much time to celebrate its eventual victory over the blockade because, like a hydra with 100 heads, the International Monetary Fund, the World Bank, an unequal rate of exchange, the brain drain of these three decades and other problems, similar or worse, are waiting for it on the other side of the U.S. siege.

THE UNITED STATES: NORMALIZATION OR REESTABLISHMENT OF RELATIONS?

Can there possibly be a more dangerous threat than that of direct subversion and the blockade imposed by the United States? Probably. Washington, in its obstinate aggressive obsession with Cuba, in spite of the six years that have already passed since the fall of the Berlin wall, has shown the world that it does not base its policy toward the island on the Truman Doctrine's idea of the containment of communism, but rather on the Monroe Doctrine which asserts its imperial right to what it considers its backyard.

In this context, the eventual reestablishment of relations with Cuba is *not* equivalent to the normalization of relations between the United States and the island. No one today in Washington questions the ultimate objective of U.S. policy toward Cuba: to overthrow the revolution and rebuild, not just "capitalism," but a brand of capitalism dominated and controlled politically and economically by the United States.

Cuba wishes to have normal relations with the United States, just like the relations it maintains with Canada, Western Europe or Japan. However, unless the United States renounces its present objective with regard to Cuba, the reestablishment of relations would not be equivalent to their normalization ("peaceful co-existence"), but to continuing the war by other means.

What is being debated today in the United States is not the goals of its Cuba policy, but the choice of the most effective instrument for attaining these goals: the intensification of the blockade and open subversion or a shift to "friendly" subversion of the island. It is not normalization of relations which is the subject of the debate today, but their gradual reestablishment in such a way as to progressively shift the emphasis from blockade and harassment to a medium and long-term policy of co-optation that would facilitate a peaceful evolution of Cuba's economic and political system reconstituted under U.S. control.

Cuban society, whose organizational design proved so effective in confronting open subversion in the previous international environment, will find it very difficult to survive this new strategy of co-optation unless radical structural changes are made to confront it. Here we return to our point of departure: Cuba urgently needs changes and a transition to another organizational model for its development, but what kind of transition and what kind of model?

The United States would prefer, if it is at all possible, a peaceful transition of Cuba toward the past, to reestablish its old sex playground in a country with a dependent economy, a submissive government and an army committed to the defense of free enterprise (especially of a transnational nature).

Cuba must move toward the future if it wishes to avoid a return to the past, and this fact, as in 1961, raises the questions: what is the nature of that authentic and economically viable socialism toward which it aspires to move, and how does it get there from this combined conjunctural and structural crisis?

Now and then, some of yesterday's mimics reappear as today's "pragmatists." Yesterday the Soviet road offered, according to them, all the security of a proven experiment. Today — according to their new model — liberal deregulation of the market, without changes in the operation of the political system, is the formula that seems to enthuse them. Their previous "pro-Sovietism" has turned into a sudden euphoria with the supposed "Chinese model," without their ever having ceased to be dogmatists. Some technocrats are also to be found, demoralized spiritually and employing a similarly pragmatic logic (but only in relation to their personal interests), who urge and defend those changes which assure them of a soft landing as managers of joint enterprises with foreign capital.

On the other hand, the United States is again pointing an accusing finger at Fidel Castro, but this time not for his revolutionary spirit but for an alleged "conservative immobility" with which he supposedly blocks and delays the above-mentioned "solutions" proposed by their so-called "reformist" colleagues. The Pentagon has even entertained the possibility of "accepting" his remaining as the head of our country if he himself takes charge of dismantling the Cuban system. "Castro without Castroism" (or rather, "Castro in the service of the restoration of capitalism"), they seem to suggest might turn out to be a negotiable and even desirable compromise.

It is a fact that Cuba today already exhibits considerable changes over the Cuba of five years ago, as the country is forced to exist in a dramatically different international context. This new reality is accelerating the rate at which concepts, instruments and styles of government are becoming obsolete. Even if they proved effective in the past, today they are increasingly inappropriate and even counterproductive. It is precisely those changes which have led an elitist sector in the United States to think that a policy of gradual co-optation would be much more effective and less risky than the intensification and extension of the blockade, which some Republican legislators are again proposing.

Internationally, certain events have had a serious impact on Cuban life in recent years. These include:

- the collapse of the Eastern bloc and the consequent crisis of the Soviet model;
- the appearance of new telecommunications technologies (faxes, electronic mail, direct dialing via satellite);
- the rapidly growing Cuban tourist industry which hopes to attract more than a million annual visitors in the next three to five years (1 for every 12 inhabitants); and
- the permanent exposure to television and radio broadcasts originating in the United States.

Internally, there are also new factors that are producing a qualitative change in the Cuba social scene such as:

- the increasing internationalization of personal and institutional life (via tourism, the new telecommunications technologies, work-related trips, increasingly frequent exchanges and contacts with Cubans residing abroad and the possibility of temporarily working abroad);
- the reappearance of a foreign and national private sector (which permits people, if they so desire, to leave their jobs with state-run enterprises and in so doing end their contact with the highly politicized Cuban labor and community environment in order to work on their own);
- the fragmenting of the internal market into two sectors: one operating with dollars (people connected with tourism, who travel or who receive remittances from abroad) with access to consumer products which are quite ordinary but which symbolize luxury in the midst of generalized scarcity, and another sector of considerable size which subsists basically on a salary which lacks buying power except for the purchase of products which are rationed and subsidized by the state; and
- the reappearance of some degree of inequality between those who have succeeded in getting high-income jobs or

who receive dollars in some way and those who have to subsist on rationing and the limited market that operates with Cuban pesos.

Ordinary citizens can observe on all sides the deterioration of the just world that they built and paid for with constant mobilizations and efforts over more than three decades.

Technocrats scramble for posts as "managers" in the mixed sector of the economy linked to foreign capital, capable engineers prefer to fix domestic appliances or drive taxis, young people prostitute themselves to obtain access to discotheques and hotels while news broadcasts and newspapers continue reflecting small daily victories in language apparently with no connection to the daily hardships which overwhelm the average citizen during this "special period" in times of U.S. blockade and hostility.

The societies that seemed to be such a firm launching pad toward the future have collapsed along with the Berlin wall and the ideological faith which in the past served to stir the population's will to sacrifice during these three decades. Increasingly now it is necessary to persuade rather than convoke. In this way a crisis in values is opening up in certain sectors of the population while Uncle Sam tries to fish in these troubled waters with more than 15 radio stations that broadcast propaganda from Miami to the island 24 hours a day. Average citizens are thus forced to search for the truth somewhere between the apologetic local press and the slander beamed at them from Miami.

CUBA FACING THE 21ST CENTURY
The world that observes Cuba is not exempt from its own challenges and crises.

The erosion and salinization of arable land, deforestation, pollution of air and water, the deterioration of the ozone layer, global warming, the rapid reduction of biodiversity, the destruction of ecosystems, acid rain and other disasters are only a few of the problems created by humankind in 200 years of industrial civilization. They are linked to patterns of consumption and unsustainable life-styles spread throughout the world by modern advertising in the context of a totally asymmetrical distribution of wealth, to which we must add the fact that the world's population promises to increase at the rate of one billion new inhabitants per decade after the year 2000.

Fifteen years of neoliberal economic policies have increased the wealth of an ever smaller number of people and the poverty of an ever greater number, at the same time that the deregulation of these policies has permitted an ever greater destruction of our natural habitat in order to maximize profits. Drug trafficking, violence, massive migrations, uncontrolled epidemics, civil wars, anarchical terrorism and other social ills are spreading all over the globe, while the mass media and the intellectual circles which support the policies in vogue exhort people toward hedonism, social demobilization and selfishness as the indispensable tools for survival, in the midst of rampant social Darwinism.

"Success" is the attainment of "power." Power to dominate others, not to serve them. Power to exploit others, not to help them. Power, in this period in which the supposed "End of History" has been proclaimed, is symbolized today — much more than ever before — by unlimited acquisition, possession and consumption. Postmodern happiness consists in the consumption of any and all merchandise (from sex to real estate). However, Kurt Cobain's suicide indicates that even those who achieve the highest levels of consumption and are themselves successful merchandise in the global celebrity market may encounter the devastating spiritual emptiness at the core of this useless and treacherous vision of the meaning of life. The appearance of organizations of entrepreneurs — such as the Social Venture Network in the United States and Europe — in which many of its members prefer to preserve the ecological balance, use cooperative, shared-management techniques and become involved in actions of social responsibility shows that, even in bourgeois sectors, there is a growing awareness that money is not everything and that human life requires social meaning.

Considering that it is the philosophy of free markets and liberal democracy which serves as the functional structure for this alienated world, it should not be so surprising that the revolutionary Fidel Castro — and many of us with him — should act in a conservative manner when it comes to evaluating which changes should now be introduced into the Cuban reality, as well as the rate and direction of change. The supposed "solutions" that are being recommended to Cuba by the Organization of American States have been successful only to the degree that they have produced the economic "miracle" of plunging nearly half the population of Latin America into abysmal poverty within only one decade.

To be conservative in Cuba today does not mean, unequivocally and automatically, to be reactionary or dogmatic. At times we act in a conservative manner precisely because we think and feel as revolutionaries. There are things in Cuba today that we wish to preserve, precisely because they constitute revolutionary values in this world dominated by reactionary logic. To be dogmatic is to think that the model of a bureaucratic, hierarchical, authoritarian, over-centralized, micro-administrative and hyper-regulatory state will provide the way out of our present crisis and preserve those precious ethical values of solidarity, independence and social justice which are being threatened today.

Humanity has spent a good part of the 20th century moving away from the myth of the market combined with liberal democracy to the myth of the bureaucratic state and vice versa, without finding the way to achieve, completely and fully, the unfulfilled promise of modern times: equality, liberty and fraternity. Not all those who propose changes are anti-dogmatic, nor are all their proposals revolutionary. There are proposals for reactionary changes fostered by people whose recent dogmatism has been simply exchanged for another of a different kind.

The people of Eastern Europe were trapped by the false dichotomy between two reactionary options with differing class structures: capitalism or "actually existing socialism" (i.e., either the free market or the bureaucratic state as the regulator for the distribution of goods, services and human rights). The most recent elections in those countries appear to indicate that the people — without wishing to return to a past marked by repressive authoritarianism and an omnipresent state — have come to understand that they put their eggs in the wrong basket when they opted for capitalism. It is regrettable that an option that is an authentic alternative to the past and present of those peoples has not appeared there, either.

Finally, in what sense are most of us Cubans conservative? What is it we wish to preserve? It is, quite simply, the nation with independence and social justice that Martí promised us and the revolution made possible and the ethic of solidarity from which our identity as Cubans and the nation itself emerged.

What is, then, the real challenge facing us? To formulate with the greatest urgency — using imagination, faith and prudence — a development model which is an alternative to capitalism and "actually existing socialism." In the last analysis, Cuba's challenge is the same humanity faces as a whole (as shown by the declaration of more than 2,000 nongovernmental organizations at the last Summit for Social Development in Copenhagen), the only difference being that we Cubans have to face it from a doubly critical situation in which time is working against us. If we do not find the solution in time we will lose, not only everything we have achieved during these years, but almost certainly our very independence and suffer a progressive erosion of our national identity (as has already occurred in Puerto Rico, or even worse). Some technocrats who, rhetoric aside, regard our reality with disillusioned cynicism, together with those always exalted pragmatists of whatever dogmatism is currently fashionable, are disturbed by the fact that Fidel Castro's supposed "conservatism" is making it difficult for them to introduce their proposals with the speed that the times do in fact demand. Nevertheless, if delaying changes in the present state of affairs will lead to certain disaster, accelerating the catastrophe with false solutions (as occurred in Eastern Europe) does not seem very sensible, either. Of course, neither the fact that the changes that some people suggest will not be accepted because of their reactionary nature nor the danger that a rapid rate of change presents to our social stability shall serve as a pretext for a dogmatic immobility on the assumption that by working "harder," everything will be resolved.

Cuba cannot — if it wishes to survive — be a museum for a dying socialism, but neither can it be the pastiche of Latin America's tragedy. Cuba has the human and material potential, in spite of the crisis, to become a successful social laboratory for a new model of authentically human and sustainable development. If it is possible to "reinvent" socialism anywhere, then the conditions for doing so exist on this island.

Thanks to the millions of dollars invested throughout these three decades in education and the creation of an infrastructure for research and development of "state of the art" technologies, Cubans can today hope for the future. With less than 2 percent of the population of Latin America, Cuba provides 15 percent of the region's scientists and technicians. More than tourism, mining or any other traditional export, the sector of high technology (mainly biotechnology and software production) is bound to become the main pillar of the future Cuban economy, inserted competitively in the information age.

Cuban society can overcome its "special period," but no one can tell us today when or how the already excessively long Latin American "special period" will come to an end.

Of course, slogans aside, there is no certain victory for the revolution. Lloyds of London would not offer an insurance policy on this prospect. But its victory — which means preserving independence and social justice within a framework of ethical solidarity — is still possible. Its most dangerous adversaries are not, however, the U.S. marines, but the false doors toward the future offered by certain naive or ill-intentioned individuals (both Cuban and foreign), as well as those who barricade themselves behind outdated, obsolete and dogmatic concepts to defend themselves from the aforementioned individuals.

Some Cubanologists claim that they distinguish two lines of thought on the island, which they term "conservative" or "modernizing," according to their fancy. Following these criteria, the "modernizers" (who doesn't like to be called that?) are those people who are prepared to make changes directed toward bringing the Cuban political system and economy in line with those of the rest of the world (i.e., free markets plus liberal democracy). Accordingly, a "conservative" is anyone who opposes such changes to the present system. The truth is that both in the description of the differences as well as the labels they hang on them are mistaken. Today the points of view on our reality can be grouped as follows:

- those who think that a greater effort, within the same structures and concepts, is the only reliable way to overcome the crisis and who hold to this criterion dogmatically;
- those who — whether or not they recognize it in their conscience and discourse — prefer to adopt a technocratic criterion and put to one side any political or social consideration in order to undertake only those changes which will strengthen the economy as the supposed main pillar for state power (not a few people support this inconsistent technocratic pragmatism as a natural rejection of the first group); and
- those of us who believe that the perceptions and proposals of the two previous groups will only lead us to a crisis in the short term (in the case of the dogmatists) or to the adulteration of the socialist revolutionary project in the medium term (in the case of the technocrats). We believe that the road to finding the solutions to our problems lies in a broad and pluralistic debate that will revive the "process of rectification" in search of a new, holistic and coherent model for development, a model which will prove to be a true alternative to both the Soviet model and capitalist society because of its genuine democratic and humanist nature within the framework of a mixed economy. This current of opinion recognizes economic viability as a prerequisite for the survival of the revolutionary project, but it does not reduce it to that factor alone, which makes its program for change essentially different from that of the technocrats.

As might be expected, each of these currents of opinion believes that the other two are "completely" mistaken (something which is not only quite human, but also typically Cuban). The revolution will have to be much more pluralistic, democratic and flexible than in the past when the time comes to define the new consensus within which — for the third time — these currents of revolutionary thought will have to integrate themselves and coexist, united in their diversity. On this occasion all of them share the feeling that, given the critical circumstances in which humanity is living today, history will not give us another chance to rectify if we take the wrong road now. This makes everyone a bit more intolerant than in past debates, precisely when we need to be more tolerant and flexible, not simply in order to hear, but also to truly listen to and consider the opinions of all of those with whom we are not in agreement.

For Cuba to be able to save its independence, social justice and ethic of solidarity— more than ever before — it will have to be Martí's Republic "with all and for the good of all."

It will not be a proliferation of political parties but the broadest possible pluralism that will unleash our collective and creative imagination. It is not the privatization but the socialization of the management of state property, today administered bureaucratically, which can restore our faith in the future. It is not the anarchic destabilization of our reality but its gradual — and timely — transformation, which can assure the possibility of our future victory. It is not the financial or bureaucratic manipulation of civil society but its still greater autonomous and participatory activity and decision making from which a new and democratic culture will emerge. It is not the free market and representative democracy but democratic planning and participatory political democracy — within the solid framework of a lawful state — which can ensure the operation and full enjoyment for everyone of their political, civil, economic, social and cultural rights. It will not be the philosophy of consumerism but that of the quality of life which will make possible an ecologically sustainable and socially responsible human development. It is not the ethic of "having" but the ethic of "being" which today can lead us out of the labyrinth in which not only Cuba, but all of humanity finds itself.

This is why Cuba's destiny is relevant to the rest of the world.

Havana, Cuba
July 9, 1995

Cuba Travel Seminars

Global Exchange organizes monthly educational seminars to Cuba examining topics such as public health, sustainable agriculture, women's issues, and the political and economic situation. These trips, which are usually 10 days long, give participants a rich understanding of both the negative and positive features of Cuba's revolution.

All trips spend some time in Havana and some time in other parts of the island. Another distinctive feature of our trips is personalized attention: in addition to daytime group activities, we try to accommodate individual requests in evening sessions that are mainly held in Cuban homes. Most trips are $1200: price includes roundtrip airfare from Miami, double accommodations, visas, all transportation in Cuba, breakfast and dinner each day, translation of all programs and reading materials.

If you are interesting in joining one of these tours, call us at (415)255-7296.

Sample themes include:

Agriculture & Sustainable Development

Cuba's Bicycle Revolution

Women's Delegation

The Cuban Economy at a Crossroads

Public Health in Cuba

Afro-Cuban Culture

Cuba in a Changing World

In addition to the monthly thematic tours listed above, Global Exchange can also organize tours to Cuba designed specifically for your organization.

Global Exchange, 2017 Mission St., Rm. 303, San Francisco, CA 94110
(415) 255-7296, FAX(415)255-7498, E-mail: globalexch@igc.org

Also from Ocean Press

CHE GUEVARA READER
Writings on Guerrilla Strategy, Politics and Revolution
Edited by David Deutschmann
The most complete selection of Guevara's writings, letters and
speeches available in English. As the most authoritative collection
to date of the work of Guevara, this book is an unprecedented
source of primary material on Cuba and Latin America in the 1950s
and 1960s.
ISBN 1-875284-93-1

CHE — A MEMOIR BY FIDEL CASTRO
Preface by Jesús Montané
Edited by David Deutschmann
For the first time Fidel Castro writes with candor and affection of his
relationship with Ernesto Che Guevara, documenting his extra-
ordinary bond with Cuba from the revolution's early days to the final
guerrilla expeditions to Africa and Bolivia.
ISBN 1-875284-15-X

CHE IN AFRICA
Che Guevara's Congo Diary
by William Gálvez
Che in Africa is the previously untold story of Che Guevara's "lost
year" in Africa. Che Guevara disappeared from Cuba in 1965 to
lead a guerrilla mission to Africa in support of liberation movements.
The story behind the Congo mission is now revealed, reprinting
Guevara's previously unpublished Congo Diary.
ISBN 1-876175-08-7

CHE GUEVARA AND THE FBI
U.S. political police dossier on the Latin American
revolutionary
Edited by Michael Ratner and Michael Steven Smith
A Freedom of Information case succeeded in obtaining Che
Guevara's FBI and CIA files, which are reproduced in this book.
These sensational materials add to suspicions that U.S. spy
agencies were plotting to assassinate Guevara in the 1960s.
ISBN 1-875284-76-1

Also from Ocean Press

CIA TARGETS FIDEL
The secret assassination report
Only recently declassified and published for the first time, this
secret report was prepared for the CIA on its own plots to
assassinate Cuba's Fidel Castro.
ISBN 1-875284-90-7

SALVADOR ALLENDE READER
Chile's Voice of Democracy
Edited with an introduction by James D. Cockcroft
This new book makes available for the first time Salvador Allende's
voice and vision of a more democratic, peaceful and just world.
ISBN 1-876175-24-9

DEADLY DECEITS
My 25 Years in the CIA
By Ralph W. McGehee
A new, updated edition of this classic account of the CIA's deeds
and deceptions by one of its formerly most prized recruits.
ISBN 1-876175-19-2

CUBA AND THE UNITED STATES
A Chronological History
By Jane Franklin
This chronology relates in detail the developments involving the two
neighboring countries from the 1959 revolution through 1995.
ISBN 1-875284-92-3

PSYWAR ON CUBA
The declassified history of U.S. anti-Castro propaganda
by Jon Elliston
Secret CIA and U.S. Government documents are published here for
the first time, showing a 40-year campaign by Washington to use
psychological warfare and propaganda to destabilize Cuba.
ISBN 1-876175-09-5

Also from Ocean Press

AFROCUBA
An anthology of Cuban writing on race, politics and culture
Edited by Pedro Pérez Sarduy and Jean Stubbs
What is it like to be Black in Cuba? Does racism exist in a
revolutionary society that claims to have abolished it? *AfroCuba*
looks at the Black experience in Cuba through the eyes of the
island's writers, scholars and artists.
ISBN 1-875284-41-9

SLOVO
The unfinished autobiography of ANC leader Joe Slovo
A revealing and highly entertaining autobiography of one of the key
figures of the African National Congress. As an immigrant, a Jew, a
communist and guerrilla fighter — and white — few public figures in
South Africa were as demonized by the apartheid government.
ISBN 1-875284-95-8

PRIEST AND PARTISAN
A South African journey of Father Michael Lapsley
by Michael Worsnip
The story of Father Michael Lapsley, an anti-apartheid priest who
became the target of a South African letter bomb attack in 1990 in
which he lost both hands and an eye.
ISBN 1-875284-96-6

I WAS NEVER ALONE
A Prison Diary from El Salvador
By Nidia Díaz
Nidia Díaz (born María Marta Valladares) gives a dramatic and
inspiring personal account of her experience as a guerrilla
commander during El Salvador's civil war. Seriously wounded, she
was captured in combat by Cuban-exile CIA agent Félix Rodríguez.
Nidia Díaz was the FMLN's Vice-Presidential candidate in 1999.
ISBN 1-876175-17-6

Also from Ocean Press

JOSE MARTI READER
Writings on the Americas
An outstanding new anthology of the writings, letters and poetry of one of the most brilliant Latin American leaders of the 19th century.
ISBN 1-875284-12-5

FIDEL CASTRO READER
The voice of one of the 20th century's most controversial political figures — as well as one of the world's greatest orators — is captured in this new selection of Castro's key speeches over 40 years.
ISBN 1-876175-11-7

CUBAN REVOLUTION READER
A Documentary History
Edited by Julio García Luis
An outstanding anthology presenting a comprehensive overview of Cuban history and documenting the past four decades, highlighting 40 key moments in the Cuban Revolution up to the present day.
ISBN 1-876175-10-9
Also available in Spanish (ISBN 1-876175-28-1)

LATIN AMERICA: FROM COLONIZATION TO GLOBALIZATION
Noam Chomsky in conversation with Heinz Dieterich
An indispensable book for those interested in Latin America and the politics and history of the region.
ISBN 1-876175-13-3

WASHINGTON ON TRIAL
Cuba's $181 billion claim against the U.S. government for war crimes
Introduced by Michael Ratner and David Deutschmann
ISBN 1-876175-23-0

Ocean Press, GPO Box 3279, Melbourne 3001, Australia
● Fax: 61-3-9329 5040 ● E-mail: edit@oceanpress.com.au

www.oceanbooks.com.au